MW01517265

MY LIFE:

Mysteries and Achievements

Ellias Ngugama

AuthorHouse™
1663 Liberty Drive
Bloomington, IN 47403
www.authorhouse.com
Phone: 1-800-839-8640

© 2013 Ellias Ngugama. All rights reserved.

No part of this book may be reproduced, stored in a retrieval system, or transmitted by any means without the written permission of the author.

Published by AuthorHouse 5/28/2013

ISBN: 978-1-4817-4934-3 (sc)
ISBN: 978-1-4817-4932-9 (hc)
ISBN: 978-1-4817-4933-6 (e)

Library of Congress Control Number: 2013908088

Any people depicted in stock imagery provided by Thinkstock are models, and such images are being used for illustrative purposes only.
Certain stock imagery © Thinkstock.

Because of the dynamic nature of the Internet, any web addresses or links contained in this book may have changed since publication and may no longer be valid.

The views expressed in this work are solely those of the author and do not necessarily reflect the views of the publisher, and the publisher hereby disclaims any responsibility for them.

TABLE OF CONTENTS

INTRODUCTION

In my life, I have enjoyed several things that Almighty God kindly opened up for me. I was the last born to my mother, who produced four sons and two daughters, and I also desired to have children, either boys or girls, when I grew up.

In September 1963, I married Theresa Erica Madyara, who came from Mhondoro District in Mashonaland, Zimbabwe. Her family is of a Shona-speaking tribe called Zezurus. I myself am Sotho, originally from South Africa. My family settled in Shurugwi District of the Midland Province in Zimbabwe. Most tribes in this district spoke a dialect of Shona called Karanga, whereas those from Theresa's province spoke Zezuru Shona.

I was so pleased to have three daughters with Theresa:

> Thandazani Gladys was born on 26 June 1964.
>
> Nomsa Theodora was born on 30 April 1967.
>
> Bongani Constance was born on 20 January 1970.

I was also extremely pleased to be blessed with my only granddaughter, born to my last daughter, Bongani. My granddaughter, Malaika Emmanuella, was born on 18 August 1997.

All three of my children pleased me very much during their education, as they all obtained various university degrees, which helped them to obtain reasonable employment and to enjoy their lives. I sincerely thank Theresa for giving me such great gifts.

My granddaughter, Malaika, also pleases me by working hard in school each day, and she is now in Grade 10. She is an "A" student in most of her subjects and on most of her projects at an excellent, highly rated secondary school. I pray that she continues to excel as she completes her secondary education and begins her university studies.

I wish to conclude my introduction by stressing that now, at my old age, I am very pleased by the closeness, love, and happiness my entire family enjoys.

—Ellias Godfrey Ngugama

ONE

Mysteries Encountered in My Early Childhood

I was born on 7 April 1940, in a small rural village in Shurugwi, a district of the Midlands Province in Rhodesia, which is now Zimbabwe. I am the youngest of six children, two girls and four boys. My parents were primarily peasant farmers. My father was regarded as one of the few well-to-do people in the village because he owned many cattle, sheep and goats and five six-wheel wagons. Rural Africans regarded these items as signs of wealth in those days because African people rarely had money in banks.

Life in the village was very simple, with very strong values of kinship. I do not remember a day my mother ever threatened to spank me for doing something untoward or unethical when I was a little boy. Instead, she gave me a look one eyebrow raised and her mouth set in a hard line suggested that I was playing in an unacceptable manner and that I needed to change my behaviour. Years later, when I became a father, I tried to apply the same normative techniques with my own children, as they were growing up in an affluent society in Canada. It did not work. Any suggestive look at any of my children would be met with, "Why are you looking at me like that?" I would never raise such a question with my mother. I quickly realized that it was I who needed to change my reaction to my children in some cases, without losing the responsibility for the proper upbringing of my children. Successfully managing this generation gap was an awesome task indeed.

In Shurugwi, soccer was the favourite pastime for small boys, and we played daily around our homes or in the bush while herding cattle. Since we had no money to buy balls, we had to improvise by collecting pieces of torn cloth and bundling them together to make a big round ball to kick around as a soccer ball. I looked forward to getting together with my friends to play soccer each day until I reached school age.

By the end of 1945, when I was 5 years old, my father had already lost his eyesight, nobody in my family knew what caused his blindness and had unsuccessfully tried all the conventional medical treatments available to Blacks in clinics and hospitals in Rhodesia at that time. It must have been painful for my family to accept that my father would probably spend the rest of his life as a blind man. He also probably found it hard to accept that. However, that is what happened. He died, years later, as a blind man.

One late afternoon in 1945, my father called me aside to speak to me privately. He insisted that I should not disclose to anybody what he was about to tell me. Naturally I agreed, even though I did not know what he was talking about. He then told me that he and I would have to go somewhere very far from home for a while. I asked, "When?" and he replied, "Now." I then secretly collected an extra shirt and pair of shorts, and we were off. He then instructed me to travel west from our home. I led him by the hand as we started on our journey. There were no clearly visible roads to follow, only the narrow paths created by cattle as they roamed to better pastures. After we had travelled for some time, my father asked me to locate a tree with low branches. I did. He then asked me to bring him close to that tree so that he could cut off a branch. He pruned the branch and asked me to hold one end of the stick while he held the other end. This made our travel along those narrow paths much easier, as I was able to lead him from a longer distance.

When we had been away from our rural village for several hours, I told my father that I was tired and that it was getting dark, so I could no longer see clearly where we were going. He then said, "Very well. Just locate a large tree nearby." "I can see a big tree in front of us," I said. "We will sleep under that tree tonight," he said with relief, as I suppose he, too, needed a rest. We both crawled into the heavy dark green overcoat that he always carried, and we fell asleep. Even though we had not had lunch or supper, I slept soundly, maybe because I was very tired.

The morning brightness woke me up. I told my father that the sun was coming up. He then said, "We must now continue our journey." So we did. As we continued our walk, my father asked, "Can you see any villages anywhere?" I replied, "Yes, there is one at some distance." At that point, he stressed to me, "You must never pass through any village or stop in one to rest or to ask for food to eat. We must pass every village at a distance." I followed these instructions to the letter.

We walked for three days, mostly in the forest, sleeping under trees each night. Along the paths he directed me to follow were plenty of wild fruit trees, especially ones called *mihacha* in the Shona language. The fruits from these trees were very sweet and filling, and my father and I lived on them during our journey.

Towards late afternoon on the fourth day, we arrived at a mountain. My father directed me to lead him to the mountain's northern side. As we approached the mountain, I saw a huge pool that I thought was a dam reservoir. My father told me to keep moving in the same direction until we got to the river that emptied into the pool, just a little farther north. The river was very shallow, so my father decided that we would cross the river at that point. As we reached the other side, we were met by a very fat woman dressed in black. She greeted us as if she were expecting us and took us to where she lived. There was no house, just tree branches stuck around a big tree, and no children or other people. The woman lived there all by herself in the middle of a thick forest. I was a bit scared at first, but because I was with my father, my fear gradually subsided. Nearby was another big tree. The strange fat woman, whose name I never learned but whom I shall call Sango, said to my father and me, "There is where you will sleep," pointing to the other big tree. Strange as it may seem, that big tree was to become our home for the next three years.

When we met Sango, I got the impression that she and my father had never met before, yet she behaved as though she had been waiting for us to arrive. There was no telephone communication that my father could have used to say how long our journey would take and precisely when we would arrive at the river crossing. Yet she was by the riverside when we arrived. Looking back now, years later, I can only conclude as a Christian that some mighty force was at play here. On our first night with Sango, Just as we had done for the last three nights, my father and I bundled ourselves into his heavy dark-green overcoat under the large tree and went to sleep.

In time, we adjusted to life with our strange host. Our new home was a little village for three people: one strange fat woman, Sango; a blind man; and a small 5-year-old boy. Sango provided and cooked food for all of us. She enjoyed drinking tea three times a day, and she baked bread rolls, which she called "fat cooks," for breakfast every day. I always wondered where Sango obtained flour, sugar and cans of condensed milk in the middle of the jungle.

On Friday afternoon, after we had finished our afternoon tea, Sango said to my father, "Tomorrow you will remain here alone while Ellias and I go to get food supplies."

My father replied, "Very well; you can go."

So very early the following morning, Sango woke me up and we started on what was for me a very long journey to an isolated store outside of the forest we lived in. As we travelled, I often failed to keep up with Sango's pace. I suspect that she periodically reduced her speed to ensure that I remained in sight and did not get lost in the thick forest. Towards noon, we arrived at a small store, having seen no villages at all along the journey. There were also no villages close to this little store. Inside was a middle-aged man and nobody. Without too much talking, Sango placed her order for the groceries she needed, and the storekeeper quickly packed them into small bags. Sango got me a bottle of Coca-Cola and a packet of biscuits to eat. My energy was restored, and within minutes, we were back on the road to return to our forest village. We got home towards sunset. My father was lying beside our tree house, alone. Thinking about it now, it amazes me that my blind father spent the whole day alone, without food or drink, in that thick forest filled with wild animals. I can only say that he remained safe through the grace of God.

After dinner that same evening, Sango said, "Ellias, you have now seen where we get our food supplies. From now on, you will go to the store to get our food once every two weeks." The timing of Sango's instructions was rather unfortunate. I was very tired after the long day's walk. For me to imagine myself going to that store alone every two weeks, carrying the heavy load alone through the thick forest, was too much to take. This was the only time that I ever thought of running away. However, I quickly dismissed that thought because I could never leave my father behind. Wherever my father was, there I would be, I thought.

Time went by fast. Two weeks were up. I now had to face my first trip to the store alone. Sango woke me up very early in the morning, gave me a piece of paper that she told me to hand to the storekeeper, and I was off. I followed the path Sango and I had travelled before, sometimes running and other times walking. The only fear I had was taking the wrong path and getting lost. Looking back now, I realize that Sango never gave me money with which to buy the groceries; she gave me only that small piece of paper to give to the storekeeper. For the next three years, I would travel to the store alone. Never did I feel as tired of walking and strained by the heavy load of groceries as I did when I went to the store with Sango the first time. It scares me now to think about the strange phenomenon of a small boy traveling alone over so many miles, carrying such a heavy load, but I never felt tired or stressed. As a matter of fact, as the years went by, I rather looked forward to my Saturday shopping trips, even though I never met anybody on the way or at the store except the storekeeper. I subsequently concluded that the store was probably closed on Saturdays, which was why I never saw anybody when I went there myself.

I experienced several very strange, close to miraculous, happenings while living in the forest with my father and Sango. Each day my father and I spent many hours lying on the sand by the big pool. Frequently, I would call out to my father to tell him of the many things I saw on the water, on the sand, and all around us. I've never told anybody else in my family about these things—not my mother, my sisters, or my older brothers. My father never told me not to tell anybody about these happenings; I just did not until now.

On several occasions, I saw women with long hair and brown skin sitting on the water apparently knitting something with white and black beads. Perhaps they sat on partially submerged rocks in the pool, but I never saw these rocks. These women often sat with their legs crossed, as ladies often do in a living room. If one such woman was alone, she would smile at me but never say anything to me. I told my father of this, and all he said was, "Go on with your playing and leave her alone." At other times, I would see one or two very large black bulls walking on the water close to the opposite bank from where we lay in the sand. On few occasions, these bulls bellowed loudly and then disappeared into the water.

At other times, I saw a number of mostly black hens and chicks near where my father and I lay in the sand. Again my father told me not to worry or chase them.

One day when my father and I were at the pool, we both fell asleep. When I woke up, I saw that a big snake like a python had encircled us. I was petrified. I screamed so loudly that my father woke up and asked me what was wrong. I explained to him, trembling, that we were encircled by a very large snake and that I could not see its head. My father then held me close to his chest and said, "Do not be afraid. The snake will not hurt us."

My trembling continued for some time as my father held me close to him. He comforted me by saying, "You should not be worried or afraid of the things that you see on or by the pool." None of the things I had seen on or by the pool frightened me except this big snake.

I can now say that I rather enjoyed seeing these happenings, and I always comfortably described them to my father as I saw them. Each time, he encouraged me to continue playing and not worry about these incidents. He never explained to me what this was all about. These mysteries were very strange to me then, and they still are now. In addition, I cannot explain the behaviour of Sango or my father during the time we lived in this forest village. Nevertheless, I am sincerely grateful to God for having exposed me to such amazing events and for blessing me with all the successes I have achieved in my lifetime.

Sango also did amazing things. Once or twice a week, Sango would walk into the deep pool to swim. I watched her sink underwater without resurfacing for a long time. The first time I saw this happen, I told my father that perhaps Sango had drowned. My father merely smiled at me and said, "Wait. She will come out soon."

After a couple of months watching Sango dip in the pool for several hours, Sango then disappeared into the pool for four or five days at a time. When she returned, she always brought back some green plants and roots from the pool. This habit went on for nearly a year and a half.

During Sango's absences from our little village, my father and I would eat only whatever food she had prepared for us before her departure, especially her fat cooks, yet my father and I never felt we were starving during her absence. Amazing, isn't it?

Looking back now, I can only assume that some strong supernatural powers controlled our environment and protected us.

For nearly two years, the rest of our immediate family did not locate our whereabouts. I later learned that they had made a missing-persons report. In those days, especially in rural African communities publicity was not as open as it is today.

Apart from the store keeper, I saw no other human beings apart from Sango and my father. Sango's disappearances into the pool for several days at a time became more frequent.

One day, a group of tribesmen brought a very sick young man on a wooden stretcher to Sango. Immediately, Sango summoned my father and asked him to heal the sick man. My father then sent me to fetch a leaf from a nearby tree. He then told me to dip the leaf into cold water in a cup and sprinkle the water over the sick man. I did that. Meanwhile, Sango sat and watched. Suddenly, the sick man jumped up and began to talk strangely and violently. At that point, Sango administered the roots and green herbs she had been collecting from the pool. She rubbed green herb on the sick man's body and washed the roots and put them in water and gave him to drink. After two days, the sick man was well and strong, and he and the tribesmen departed from our forest village.

In the third year of our stay in the forest village, a stream of people brought sick people to us who needed healing. My father and Sango spent time attending to the hundreds of sick people. Some of these people stayed for several days, but all were well when they left. My life changed because some of these people brought children with them. I now had friends to play with every day. Life was enjoyable.

Finally the news about Sango, my old man, and a 7-year-old boy, reached my family back home. A few months later, towards the end of 1947, my mother and older brothers located us. They came to our forest village. Somehow, I had not missed my mother and my brothers that much in all those years. I cannot explain why this was so. Nevertheless, it was a joy to see them after such a long time. I told my mother and older brothers that we were quite happy in our forest village and that the several hundred people they saw had only started coming there recently. As I explained our lives in the forest village, my mother started crying, and her tears continued to drop a long time. I suppose both my mother and older brothers must have felt that our life in the bush for so long was painful and regrettable, yet for my father and I, our life was liveable.

After three days, my mother and brothers returned to our home village.

To this day I do not know what they discussed with my father and Sango. My guess is that they probably expressed pleasure in seeing so many people seeking help. I do not believe that Sango or my father explained the unusual experiences that we went through over the years, and I never mentioned the scenes I had witnessed at the pool. All of my family members except my immediate older brother are now dead, having lived without ever knowing what I experienced with my blind father and Sango.

For the next several months, my mother visited us accompanied by other relatives. During each visit, my mother and older brothers asked me to return home to attend school. By then I had turned 8 years old, and they pointed out that many children my age and even younger had already started going to school. I repeatedly told my mother and my older brothers that I would not return home without my father.

Towards the middle of 1948, my father and I left Sango and our forest home to return to our home village. I began school, even though it was late in the second term.

To this day I do not know what became of Sango after we left her. My father lived for many years after we returned to our village, and he privately continued his healing. He eventually died a very energetic old man of over 90 years old.

TWO

Primary Education and Amazing Incidents

In 1948, towards the end of the second school term, I started Grade 1. I managed to catch up with the rest of my classmates. During the third term, I was made to spend more time learning with students in Grade 2. Initially, I did not understand why my class teacher and the headmaster decided to do this to me, after I had worked so hard. However, I later learned that both of them believed that my learning capacity was far ahead of other Grade 1 students, so the headmaster approached my mother to request her permission for the school to promote me to Grade 2. My mother had never been to school in her life, and she thought that with the promotion, I would miss learning many things, which might affect my progress in higher grades, so she refused to have me promoted after such a short time in Grade 1. Looking back now, I often feel that both of my parents were smarter than all their children, even though they never attended school. My parents encouraged us to study hard, and as a result, we all earned professional qualifications.

At the end of the school term or year, my mother did not ask me whether I had passed. Instead, she asked me what position I had achieved. If ever I replied that I got a position other than first position, she would ask,

"Why?" I now realize that her attitude was to motivate me to always aim for the best results in my class.

When I was in Grade 6, in a different school from the one in which I started my schooling, very strange things happened to me. For a reason I do not know, the headmaster of that school appointed me captain for the entire school. In those days, African strongly stressed strict discipline among all schoolchildren, and the school captain helped to maintain discipline throughout the school.

At that time, I was a short, 13-year-old boy, and boys and girls of 15 to 19 years of age still attended lower primary schools. Therefore, leading the whole school in assemblies and sports competitions with other schools seemed an impossible task for a 13-year-old. Whenever I addressed the entire school for a briefing, I had to climb on a wooden stool for most children to be able to see and hear me. I always instructed all school prefects to monitor enforcement of all the rules and regulations that I announced.

My first difficulties as a school captain came in achieving disciplined behaviour, especially from older boys. However, after I sent a good number of disobedient older boys to serve punishment after school a few times, they began to change their behaviour. My confidence increased, and I enjoyed the power and authority associated with my position.

Once every year, more than twenty lower primary schools in our school district would hold sports and music competitions. These competitions would last a few days at one central location, and all the students would camp out while engaging in those competitions.

Our school's headmaster was also the conductor for our choir. He composed a song about me to be sung at the music competition that year. This was a surprise for me. This headmaster was not my relative, and he did not come from my village or district. The song he composed started with my full name and then highlighted the fact that I was the captain of the whole school. It further stressed that academically, I was the most knowledgeable student in our school. What an unusual thing, I thought. This song was beautiful and touching.

One of my greatest weaknesses was my repeated failure to talk about mysterious situations I had been exposed to with my family, especially my mother. I have never known why I did that. Anyhow, my mother indicated that she would attend the schools competitions that year, 1953. Yet, I didn't inform her that our school would sing a song about me at the music competition so that she would not be surprised. Hundreds of people from the entire district, including parents, teachers and students attended these competitions.

The time came for our school choir to get on stage to present the song before a large crowd. I did not anticipate the impact a song about me would have on the crowd, especially on my mother. As the choir began to sing this song, my mother cried loudly, and the rest of the crowd was dead silent. Other parents and teachers tried to comfort her and quiet her. I can only assume that my mother was fearful that her son, her last born, would be insecure being openly publicized or that she developed strong pride in her son. I never asked her afterwards why she had cried so loud. I simply went to her and embraced her quietly, and she smiled at me.

At the conclusion of the music competition, a panel of independent judges announced the winners. Our school was awarded first prize. Naturally, I was elated and shook hands with our headmaster to thank him for composing a winning song and conducting the winning school choir.

I wish technology had been as developed in rural areas then as it is today. I might have taped that song about me so that I could play it to my granddaughter, Malaika, today. I wish to thank headmaster giving me the two greatest gifts at that primary school.

At the age of 14, I started the next stage of my school life at boarding school. My parents and my oldest brother insisted that I had to attend boarding school very far from our rural district. The journey to this school entailed an all-day bus trip, followed by an all-night train ride and finally an all-morning bus trip. The first boarding school my family wanted me to attend had not offered me a place for my senior primary education, so I was ordered to go to that school two weeks before the start of the new school year. That I did.

That school was a big Christian institution comprising senior primary school, teacher-training college (for primary school teachers) and three-year agricultural extension training. The principal was a White man, and the majority of teachers were also White. Upon my arrival at this institution, I went straight to the principal's office. He was very kind to talk to me without an appointment. After a long interview, the principal offered me a place at his institution for my senior primary education. He then told me to come back to his office the following morning. When I got to his office the next day, he told me that he would give me a job in his office starting that morning. He then said that I would not be paid for that work; however, I would receive free food and accommodation until the new school year started in two weeks' time. My duties included delivering mail to various teachers using his bicycle, cleaning his office and filing documents as directed by his secretary, who was also White. In a way, this was my introduction to office work, a great confidence-builder for my career in later years!

By the time the first term began, I had come to know nearly all teachers and boarding masters. In turn, they also seemed to have developed a liking for me. The principal continued to allow me to use his bicycle on weekends to do messenger duties for his office. This was the greatest inspiration I ever had at a boarding school.

In those days, new students to a boarding school would be teased by older students during the first week of the first term. Since I appeared to know my way around the institution and knew nearly all officials and teaching staff, I was not subjected to teasing, even though I was a new student. The two years I spent at this great Christian institution were my best years at a boarding school.

A very strange thing happened to me when I was in my second year at this wonderful institution. Due to my age and size, I was initially placed in the small-boys' dormitory. However, I continuously complained to the school captain and the boarding master that many kids in my dormitory wet the bed each night, and the smell of their blankets and mattresses caused me to sneeze frequently. The school captain later moved my bed to his room, where he lived alone, close to senior students' dormitories. This surprised me. I had expected to be moved to another dormitory, but one where there was no bedwetting. The boarding master later told me that I would enjoy privileges reserved for the senior students living near the captain's room. Residents in these quarters were teacher-training students and agricultural-extension students (the latter was the school captain's area of study). The school captain treated me just like his own younger brother. What a remarkable benefit!

One day the school captain had to go to his home district very far from the institution to attend a funeral for one of his relatives. This occasion was the first time I ever slept alone in his room. That night when I was asleep, one of the older girls from the girls' hostel came to the captain's room and carried me away. As she got to the main gate of the boys' hostels, she dropped me there. Early the following morning, the boarding master and other senior students noticed me lying by the gate, still in my pyjamas. As they were trying to wake me up, a loud noise came from the girls' hostels some distance away. One of the older girls was running around the girls' hostels naked and wouldn't stop. The principal was called to the scene. At the same time, the boys' boarding master reported my own incident. What a coincidence of strange events.

The principal then ordered that the girl be wrapped in a blanket. Since it was still the very early hours of the morning, I was dressed in my long pyjamas. The principal asked the girl to explain why she had been running around naked. She responded by saying that she had spent the whole night searching for an entrance into the girls' hostels where she lived. She further stated that she had gone to the boys' hostels to collect Ellias (me) because she wanted to eat my cheeks. I never heard why she wanted them so badly. She continued to explain that when she picked me up from my bed and carried me to the main gate, a powerful lightning strike forced her to drop me. She then ran back to the girls' hostels. However, she could not find the entrance, so she continued running all night, just to find the entrance. What an amazing incident!

The principal later summoned the girl's parents to his office, and the girl was expelled from that great institution. It took me a little while to get over what I imagined would have happened to me if this girl had succeeded in taking me to whatever place she wanted to in order to enjoy my cheeks. Fortunately, the school captain soon returned, and I no longer needed to sleep alone in his room.

During the holidays at the end of the term, I narrated this entire incident to my parents when I got home. My father quietly stressed to me that I should be grateful to the powers I could not see for the help they gave me in avoiding a terrible disaster.

I received secondary-school education at another big Christian institution very far from my home village and close to the border with Botswana. My greatest happiness at this school was getting close to my history teacher and his wife. They were both White and from the United Kingdom. The wife was the secretary to the principal of the institution. They had no children. Most weekends, the couple invited me to their house and treated me so well. I always felt that they loved me and treated me like their own son. What a blessing, I thought each time I was with them. Years later, I realized how few people, young or old, I had loved and treated as well as I was treated by this White couple, and at a time when Black people in our country were oppressed and discriminated against by Whites. I can only thank that couple most sincerely for what they did for me.

At this institution, I became friends with a young man who happened to be the younger brother of a girl who was involved with a senior prefect in teacher training. I ended up meeting both the girl and the prefect through my friend. The senior prefect was a very religious person who led prayers and gave sermons on Sundays in the villages around the institution. I used to attend these prayers and sermons. The senior prefect and the girl eventually got married. I only highlight my exposure to them because when Rhodesia gained its independence from British colonial rule in 1980, this gentleman (a reverend) became the first Non-Executive President of our independent country, now called Zimbabwe. Around that time, I was also asked to return to Zimbabwe to serve as Deputy Comptroller and Auditor-General for the Zimbabwean Government.

After secondary school, I was fortunate to enrol at a non-Christian institution in Rhodesia to study in the Commercial Courses Program of a South African college. However, this program was to be discontinued in Rhodesia after 1960, the year I enrolled, and the institution consolidated the three-year program into one year. We had to attend lectures seven days a week, and we were not allowed to participate in extracurricular activities like sports as our time to study was very tight. I was very lucky to complete the program with first-class passes in most of my subjects.

THREE

My First Employment and Political Activities

In November 1960, Roan Selection Trust, a large mining company involved in mining operations in Botswana, Zambia and Rhodesia, reviewed the progress of students in my commercial class to identify prospective employees for its head office in Salisbury, Rhodesia. I was very lucky to be picked and offered the position of a bookkeeper for the company.

In interviews with RST's director of human resources, I explained that I was so deeply interested and involved in political activities against White discrimination and oppression of Black people in our country. I stressed that I would not stop my involvement with the National Democratic Party. The director told me that he would bring my views to the Chairman of RST.

I was surprised when the Chairman stressed that my intended political activities would be respected and that he would sign a separate employment agreement allowing me to continue my employment with RST and also to continue having my salary paid even if I was arrested, detained, or imprisoned for any period less than five years. I would only lose my job and pay if I were imprisoned for more than five years. I could not believe this. I was amazed by the Chairman's support for what I intended to pursue outside of my work at the company.

This support for my political intentions also surprised me because this gentleman was White, British and awarded knighthood. He certainly was one of the very few White people in Rhodesia at the time who was against oppression of the Black people. I was really amazed by his interest in me, a man of only 20 years of age. I was also one of the first African employees in RST's head office, among over 400 White employees.

When I started my employment in December 1960, I was allocated a three-bedroom house in a new Black African Township called Mufakose Township, in Salisbury, the capital city of Rhodesia. This township was still under construction. All houses were to be allocated only to married Black people. Under the Land Apportionment Act, White residential areas were segregated from those of Black people. The Chairman of RST had tried to get me a single-bedroom accommodation within the city of Salisbury, but this was prohibited, and the prohibition was confirmed by correspondence from the Prime Minister's office, which emphasized that this area was strictly for Whites. So, the Chairman found me a big house in this new Blacks-only township, even though I was not yet married. I was very lucky to be accepted into this big house, which the Chairman fully furnished before I moved in.

Within a short time of taking residence in this township, I started my political activities. I was quickly elected Youth Chairman of the town's branch of the National Democratic Party. My political activities intensified, and police arrested and detained me often. I was not imprisoned at that time because no clear evidence that I had committed an unlawful act could be submitted to court.

The National Democratic Party was then banned by the White Rhodesian regime. African political activists, including myself, were detained for days in police cells or detention camps. Without much delay, another Black African political party called Zimbabwe African People's Union (ZAPU) was formed, and Dr. Joshua Nkomo, who had been president of the banned NDP, was elected President of ZAPU.

My political activities then continued as part of ZAPU, which was to conduct fresh elections in all branches throughout the country. In the branch in the township where I lived, I was again elected Youth Chairman of ZAPU.

In 1962, while still working for RST, I won a scholarship to Cambridge University in the United Kingdom to study Business Management and Industrial Relations. I thoroughly enjoyed this program.

As I continued my work with RST, I very much enjoyed the accounting work for several mining companies that had been allocated to me. The chief accountant for the whole group, , whom I worked under was always polite to me the only black employee in his department. He taught me so much and exposed me to many senior staff members, managers and directors of the company.

At the same time, however, my political involvement against discrimination of Black people gained coverage in the news, as I often addressed rallies of thousands of people on the weekends. Sometimes police arrested me on the platform during an address and threw me into a police truck and then into a cell. At times police shot into the crowd following my arrest, killing a number of innocent people. My detentions and court appearances became more frequent. During these, police played tapes of my speeches as evidence that I had violated the Law and Order Act, but judges would not hear the evidence, and I would therefore be set free.

My business life was full of surprises. I was privileged and thrilled to be paid a "White people salary," which was unheard of for Black people then, as they were only entitled to receive "African wages." I also enjoyed the great advantage of an identity card. All Black people in Rhodesia at that time were required to always carry a National Registration Certificate, in the form of long foolscap papers giving detailed identification information. In my case, the Chairman of RST had arranged for me to be issued with an identity card, bearing my full name, my photo and an identity number. Such cards were normally issued only to White people.

When I look back at the privileges, advantages and benefits I enjoyed at this big mining company, despite my open African political activities, I can only say thank you to the Chairman of RST and to my Father in Heaven for giving me so much that I did not deserve at the time.

Notwithstanding all the privileges I enjoyed, I continued my political activities as racial discrimination and oppression of Black people deepened. This treatment prompted Black political activists to consider different, more intense methods of dealing with the White racist regime.

The Chairman of RST was uniquely forward-thinking compared to others in Rhodesia. If only 10 to 15 percent of White people in Rhodesia had possessed a similar outlook for the country's future as the Chairman, I am certain that Rhodesia would never have faced the severe military revolution that resulted in Rhodesia becoming the independent Republic of Zimbabwe.

On several occasions, the Chairman asked me to join him and some of his directors for lunch at a hotel. Nearly all hotels in Salisbury had big signs posted at the entrance saying, "Blacks and dogs not allowed." Waiters came to our table to take our orders, including mine, but they would then bring food for everybody except me. The Chairman would then ask where my meal was. The waiters, who were all Black, would quickly rush back to the kitchen without saying anything. Within few minutes, the kitchen supervisor, who was always White, would come out and say, "The hotel does not serve Blacks." The Chairman, directors and I would then leave the hotel, my companions' meals left at the table uneaten. At two small restaurants, the Chairman offered to pay their weekly income should White people stop coming because they had agreed to serve a Black person. The two restaurants agreed, and the Chairman then instructed his White employees to go to those restaurants for lunch, using company lunch vouchers to pay for their meals. Eventually, these restaurants were always full, even though a Black person was also being served among the White customers. These restaurants finally became multiracial.

I believe the Chairman was sent by God to bring about change among His children driven by Satan to discriminate against His other innocent children. We all came from the same loving father, despite our different skin colours. I pray and hope that the Chairman's soul rests in peace beside our Lord and Saviour Jesus Christ and God our Father in Heaven.

For a long time, White employees of RST wondered why I returned to work as if I had been on holiday after spending a week or two weeks in detention. Nearly all of them knew that I was active in African politics. However, I noticed a strange thing after I had been at my workplace for a long time: The majority of those White employees and managers seemed to like me. In return, I was also friendly with most of them.

This experience taught me that human beings are loving and kind. Unfortunately, those who seek political power and wealth impose conditions that discriminate against and oppress the innocent, and all others must follow if they wish to survive and run their own lives. What sad, anti-Godly behaviour!

I then decided to enrol at the University of Rhodesia and Nyasaland to pursue studies towards a diploma in Applied Economics, majoring in Economics, Law and Accounting. As I was completing my studies, I was promoted to the position of Assistant to the Group Economist and Statistician at RST. I really enjoyed working with my immediate boss. To make matters even more amazing for me, my boss, his secretary, I and my secretary were all relocated to the top floor of the tallest building in the capital city at that time. This was the floor on which the Chairman and all directors of the company also had their offices. My office was very close to the Chairman's.

In my new position, I was often involved in several reports and projects that my boss and I presented to the board of directors. I was always fascinated with my work. To have such close contact with the company's directors and the Chairman was amazing and gratifying for me.

Years later, after Zambia gained independence from British colonial rule, the Chairman decided to move RST's head office from Salisbury, Rhodesia, to Zambia. The company selected very few managers and senior employees to move to the new head office, and I was very lucky to be asked to be one of them. My white immediate boss was not asked to move, and I never knew why.

I was greatly pressured by my political involvement to stay in Rhodesia. With great pain in my heart, I declined the offer to move to Zambia. A few days after I declined, the Chairman surprised my boss and I by allowing us to continue our work in our current office in Salisbury for nearly two years. This was an amazingly kind offer. We then continued our work in Rhodesia, submitting the necessary reports to the head office in Zambia. This also enabled me to continue my political activities. The

White Rhodesian Government again banned the ZAPU political party. Following weeks of imprisonment, most political activists, including myself, were sent to court for trial. I was one of the lucky ones to be found not guilty and released because police failed to produce clear evidence and charges against me before the court.

A very clear decision had been reached shortly before the ban: ZAPU would be the last African political party to be registered in Rhodesia. Future political activities would be carried out underground. Some time after the ban of ZAPU, the People's Caretaker Council was formed by the leaders of the banned ZAPU to coordinate all our political activities as well as our struggle against the oppressive White regime in our country.

At that time, I was chosen to be the Youth Chairman for the entire Salisbury district under the Caretaker Council. It was now time for us to coordinate, underground, with our office then operating from Lusaka, Zambia, led by the vice president of the banned ZAPU in Rhodesia. It was also time for us to intensify the real African revolution in Rhodesia and use of military weapons in open warfare against the oppressive White regime.

FOUR

My Secret Escape from Rhodesia into Zambia

Following a long involvement in political activities inside Rhodesia, I was now being hunted for arrest or death. News headlines called for my arrest or capture, dead or alive. I abandoned my residence completely and spent more time in the bush. The vice president of ZAPU, now operating from Lusaka, Zambia, organized for my secret and sophisticated rescue from Rhodesia and relocation to Zambia. I was packed into a wooden box loaded underneath wooden planks being transported to Zambia. The lorry had three trucks loaded with steel and wooden planks. Hence, the oppressive White regime in Rhodesia failed to capture me or kill me.

Upon my arrival in Lusaka, I stayed at ZAPU headquarters. There, I continued to be deeply involved in our political and military struggle against the White regime in Rhodesia.

Later on, I got a job as a financial accountant for BAT Tobacco Manufacturing. I continued to participate in our political struggle as part of ZAPU.

In 1967, I enrolled in full-time studies at the University of Zambia. I graduated in 1970 with a degree in Public Administration, Sociology and Business Management. During all four years at this university, I was elected Chairman of the university's branch of ZAPU, as many students were Black Rhodesians.

Following my graduation, I joined Coopers and Lybrand, an international firm of chartered accountants, as a management accountant. I was responsible for the bookkeeping and accounting functions of the entire company, preparing financial statements at the balance sheet level and all supporting schedules. Having a position to manage the operations of several clients of Coopers and Lybrand provided me with an important building block in the development of my ability to solve issues experienced in a wide range of business operations. I thoroughly enjoyed my work at this company.

FIVE

My Government Employment in Canada and Zimbabwe

In 1972, my landed immigrant status had been approved by the Canadian Government, and I immigrated to Canada. I had never been to Canada before, but I decided to go to Edmonton, Alberta.

As I was getting ready to go to Canada, I wrote a personal letter to Canadian Prime Minister Pierre Trudeau, and indicated that I had never been to Canada so I did not know how to react if I should meet difficulties upon my arrival in Canada. He replied to my letter in his own hand advising me to contact him directly should I run into any problems upon my arrival in Canada. I could not believe that a prime minister of a developed country would respond like that to a Black African man only 32 years old. I never experienced any big problems upon my arrival in Edmonton, Alberta, but I was very lucky to shake hands with the Prime Minister when he visited Edmonton, Alberta, in later years.

Being a Catholic, I also wrote a personal letter to the Bishop of Edmonton advising him I was coming to Edmonton and noting that I had never been to Alberta before. The Bishop was so kind to me. His reply stated that he would book an accommodation at a hotel for me and that he would make sure that someone would be at the airport to take me to the hotel. What great care the Bishop gave me! What he said is exactly what happened, and I had absolutely no problems upon my arrival in Edmonton.

God loves us so much that if you sincerely open yourself up even to top dignitaries, as I did to the Prime Minister and to the Catholic Bishop, He will open doors for you. I sincerely wish to thank those two dignitaries for the kindness, love and assistance they gave me. May God bless their souls.

The morning after my arrival at the hotel, I sent out résumés to several organizations and companies that I picked up from advertisements and the telephone directory the night before.

The biggest surprise to me was that on the fourth day of my time in Edmonton, I received a call from the Alberta Social Services and Community Health Ministry for an interview. It was absolutely amazing that a government ministry would call me for an interview so soon. I was expecting to have interviews with businesses, as that was where my main experience and interests lay. I accepted to go for the interview on that day. After a rather long interview, I was offered a job as Assistant Accountant and Frontline Supervisor in the Ministry. This startled me. I was expecting to attend several job interviews before getting any offer. Nevertheless, I accepted the offer. I was then told to start work the following day, Friday, my fifth day in Canada. What an amazing blessing for me.

After a year, I was promoted to a management position, as Financial Consultant in Budgets and Forecasts, within the Ministry. I thoroughly enjoyed my work, and I had very good relations with my colleagues and workers under me. Life was so dramatically different in Canada from what I had experienced under the racist White regime in Rhodesia. I was the only Black person in a management position in the Ministry at that time, yet almost all workers, management and staff, liked me and treated me as if my skin colour was like their own. Letters I sent back to Rhodesia and to Zambia expressed my great love for Canada and its citizens. In each of them I stressed that this country would certainly be my permanent home.

During my time in Canada, I studied professional accounting and a postgraduate Bachelor of Commerce degree at the University of Alberta.

In 1980, I was then promoted to the position of Director of Finance in the Ministry of the Environment. I had overall responsibility for all financial and accounting functions in the Ministry. I continued to enjoy my work in the Alberta government. When I first started working for the government, I thought that I would do so only for a short time, as I believed that my main interest was in private business. I was wrong. I enjoyed the good relations I had with my staff, other managers and ministers. Life in the residential communities where I had bought a house was so beautiful for all of us. Even though winter was very cold, that never bothered us at all.

All the time that I worked in Alberta, I continued my political participation in ZAPU. The party was now involved in a very intensive military struggle against the racist White regime in Rhodesia. I spent time and effort collecting used clothes donated by Canadians for our refugees, children, women and wounded young militants in need of help in Zambia and Mozambique. ZAPU had now come together with Zimbabwe African National Union (ZANU), another Zimbabwe political party operating from Mozambique to form the Patriotic Front and coordinate their military struggle against the regime in Rhodesia.

Leaders in both political parties traveled around the world, visiting Canada and the United States and participating with the United Nations to highlight our struggle in Rhodesia. I assisted members of both parties by accommodating them at my home in Edmonton following their various meetings and addresses.

In 1980, Rhodesia finally became the independent of British colonial rule and formed the Republic of Zimbabwe, and discussions between myself and the Zimbabwean government started. The government requested that I return to Zimbabwe to make meaningful contributions in our government's effort to expeditiously develop our country. It took me a long time to decide whether to return. At that time, I was afraid that Zimbabwe might follow the example of several independent countries in Africa and adopt undemocratic ways of governing. However, I received very encouraging indications that the cabinet ministers of the new government were largely very educated people. This seemed to highlight that the Zimbabwean government would definitely be run more efficiently and democratically than other governments.

In 1981, I then accepted my appointment as Deputy Comptroller and Auditor-General for the Zimbabwean government. Thereafter, I submitted my three months' notice that I would be leaving my position with the Alberta government and returning to Zimbabwe.

My responsibilities in Zimbabwe involved overall management of complex audit functions, through the principal directors of audits, supported by several directors of audit and their staffs. I prepared and presented all memoranda to the Select Committee of Public Accounts in Parliament for subsequent presentation to Parliament following the committee's deliberations. I spent a lot of my time in meeting with this committee, as it reviewed and investigated various cases brought before Parliament by the Auditor-General.

In addition to my parliamentary responsibilities, I often held meetings with permanent secretaries and ministers, offering them the necessary management advice on matters relating to internal checks and controls in ministries that would ensure effective and efficient government operations. I was also often requested to give lectures to deputy secretaries and assistant deputy secretaries of all ministries to help in their development as managers. I thoroughly enjoyed these lectures, as I got a feeling that these senior government officials felt that they were gaining the knowledge they needed to effectively carry out their functions.

SIX

My High-Level Business Achievements

In October 1983, my long and successful association with the largest multinational corporation in Zimbabwe, Anglo American Corporation Zimbabwe, began when I was employed as company secretary. This was a very high position in this huge corporation, especially for someone coming from outside the corporation and without thorough knowledge of their operations. In accepting my job as Deputy Comptroller and Auditor-General for the Zimbabwe Government, I had hoped to spend no more than five years in that position. I had made enough contributions to changing management functions and developing management that I felt comfortable leaving the job at that time. Nevertheless, I regretted some comments some politicians made in Parliament following the announcement of my resignation. I sat in Parliament on the day the announcement was made and listened to these comments. I completely accepted those highlighting the point that I should have stayed for much longer to maintain the effectiveness of issues brought before Parliament, and I thanked them for that.

Within Anglo American Corporation, my career progressed rapidly. In less than a year, I was promoted to Divisional Secretary, and within the same month, I was promoted again to Anglo Manager. With immediate effect, I was appointed Director of Bindura Nickel Corporation and Director of Zimbabwe Alloys, the two largest mining companies within the group. I was also appointed Chairman of Industrial Metal Products Company, as well as Director of Clay Products, Boart Zimbabwe and Prospecting Ventures. Subsequently, I was assigned management responsibility for Iron Duke Mine. Soon after this, I was then appointed as Financial Director for Bindura Nickel Corporation and Zimbabwe Alloys. Thereafter, I was finally appointed as Managing Director of Bindura Nickel Corporation, which at the time was contributing nearly 60 percent of foreign currency revenue to the group in Zimbabwe.

My executive responsibilities in Anglo American Corporation in Zimbabwe extended to various chairmanships. I became Chairman of Anglo American Corporation Zimbabwe, Chairman of Organizational Training and Development and Hawk Ventures, and others. This was very interesting exposure indeed, and it enabled me to influence change where I felt it was necessary. Over time, the two chairmen that I served under at Anglo American were both friendly with me and open-minded. Hence, I achieved pleasant success under their leadership.

Outside Anglo American Group, I was also exposed to other activities. In 1987, I was appointed a representative of Anglo on the Chamber of Mines National Employment Council Negotiating Committee, meeting regularly with the Mine Workers Union. I was then appointed an alternate on the Chamber of Mines Executive Committee. A year later, I was elected Senior Vice President of the Zimbabwe Chamber of Mines. In this position, I took over as chairman of various committees. Finally, in 1990, I was elected the first Black president of the Chamber of Mines of Zimbabwe.

What was most interesting for me was my wide involvement in a number of companies and organizations, particularly from 1990 onwards. In addition to my fast promotions within the Anglo Group, I was also appointed to the following positions:

- Chairman of Astra Corporation Group
- Chairman of Zimbabwe Export Processing Zones Authority
- Deputy Chairman of Minerals Marketing Corporation, Zimbabwe
- Chairman of Fleming Martin Zimbabwe
- Chairman of Standard Fire and General Insurance
- Chairman of Zimbabwe Progress Fund
- Director of the Reserve Bank of Zimbabwe
- Director of Standard Chartered Bank, Zimbabwe
- Director of Innscor Africa Limited
- Director of First Mutual Life Assurance

All this exposure helped me to develop extensive knowledge of management and business skills, which assisted my performance in all the activities that I was involved in. As I look back at responses I received following several speeches I delivered in many places and different countries, I can only conclude that I must have been the most fortunate business executive of my time.

SEVEN

My Speeches on Managing Change and Human-Resource Management and Development

In an address to non-executive directors of various companies on 31 March 1998 and 11 November 1998, I stressed that to understand the role of non-executive directors in an organization would require that we look at the recommendations of the Treadway Commission in the United States as well as the Cadbury Committee in the United Kingdom.

These two committees had investigated and made recommendations relating to financial aspects of corporate governance. The Cadbury Committee primarily considered financial reporting and accountability, good practices for the responsibilities of executive and non-executive directors, the case for audit committees, the principal responsibilities of auditors and the links between shareholders, boards and auditors.

In South Africa, the King Committee was formed after the publication of the Cadbury Report. It included much wider considerations than those of the Cadbury Committee such as codes of ethics for business enterprises in South Africa. Recognising the need to split the role of the chairman and chief executive of a company, the King Report suggested that non-executive directors should provide a strong and independent element on the board.

An executive director is usually an employee of a company who fulfills executive functions, whereas a non-executive director will not be an employee of the company and will frequently be appointed only on a part-time basis. However, non-executive directors should ensure that they have sufficient time not only to attend board meetings but also to do such reading and preparation for them as is necessary to keep themselves informed about the business activities of the company and the industry in which the company is involved.

A non-executive director has the same liability and fiduciary duties to the company as any other director for loss arising from a breach of duties. For this reason, non-executive directors should ensure that they have the same access to company information as executive directors have.

It is generally accepted that shareholders elect directors to oversee the company's operations on their behalf. The directors, in turn, appoint company officers, who are responsible for day-to-day management of the company. It must therefore be accepted that the board must retain full and effective control over the company by monitoring the executive management and ensuring that decisions on material matters are in the hands of the board.

Although I have mentioned that the King Report emphasized the need for directors to report on their company's compliance with a code of corporate practices and conduct and on effectiveness of the company's system of internal controls, I nevertheless must point out that several sub-committees of the board, such as audit committees and remuneration committees, should normally employ non-executive directors as a majority of their members.

What is so great about the inclusion of non-executive directors on the board of directors of a company is that they bring wider general or special experience into board discussions, they monitor management performance against budgets and stated strategy, and they ensure that the financial and other information available to the board are adequate.

I have also noticed that in Zimbabwe, many people seeking appointment to boards as non-executive directors merely wish to have their names on company letterhead and to receive board fees. Many such people do not make meaningful contributions in the boardroom. To permit such behaviour to continue in organizations is to ignore the fundamental duties of a director in a company. Such duties, if not performed well, will affect the personal integrity of each director, whether an executive or a non-executive director.

I hope that I have clarified in your minds the very important role that non-executive directors have in an organization. Various stakeholders need the comfort that independent directors who enjoy no personal benefits from that company are available to safeguard company assets and stakeholders' interests in the company. Non-executive directors help to create that zone of confidence. However, non-executive directors have to be effective in their contributions to decisions for the company. It is not good enough to have one's name on the company letterhead. One must be completely knowledgeable about the goings-on in the company and its industry to be effective. The role of non-executive directors is guided by both structural and legal frameworks that define their duties, and these roles and duties must be afforded the seriousness they deserve.

On 12 November 1997, I gave an address to the Zimbabwe Mining

Conference called "Managing Change in the Mining Industry." The most difficult aspects of our business, social or private lives are always managing time and managing change. These phenomena become even more difficult to handle because they are situational and often influenced by both endogenous and exogenous factors.

My own thoughts on the problems of managing change in the mining industry in Zimbabwe are based largely on the fact that it is a high-risk business often requiring a medium- to long-term outlook on investing and encouraging this sector's operators. The mining industry always requires technically developed and experienced human resources to facilitate and support operational activities, and it often requires large capital investments and long lead times before significant return on those investments are realized. Combined with all these variables, thought must also be given to environmental dictates, social or political, that will directly influence the success of the mining activity to be undertaken in Zimbabwe.

Therefore, to be effective, the investor, manager, worker, trade unionist, supplier or customer needs to be able to manage change. Technology is rapidly changing. What are you doing to equip your employees or your technical staff with the necessary know-how to keep up with this change?

Political views and options available to government also change. How do you ensure that your organization has an appropriate understanding of political sentiment at a particular time? Development of trade unionism depends on various factors inside and outside your operating environment. How do you ensure full understanding and appreciation of those labour sentiments to minimize disruption to your operations?

All these factors and many others are always acting upon your organizational environment, and they require effective management if your company is to see continued success. As managers of our diverse operations, if we fail to manage change, then change will manage us. Many of us have heard of or been part of organizations in the habit of reacting to events after they occur. In such circumstances, the events manage those companies. A clear example of failure to manage change! Managing change does not necessarily guarantee desirable consequences. Instead, it means that consequences of events have been anticipated and that appropriate contingency plans have been prepared for them. That is managing change.

What are some of the tools we need to manage the change process effectively in the mining industry in Zimbabwe? First, we must have intimate knowledge of the mining industry in Zimbabwe and worldwide. Second, we must know that commodities prices in the world market will always change, favourably or adversely. Factors contributing to these price changes are usually beyond the control of Zimbabwean mineral producers, mainly because we are all price-takers in a vicious world market. How then do we prepare and motivate our employees to keep pace with the rapidly changing world of mining to ensure that our companies remain competitive? Zimbabwe's minerals are generally of a low grade and therefore costly to produce. But technology has been improving in the world of mining. Has the mining industry in Zimbabwe kept pace with that change? If it has not, how will our industry cope in the highly competitive and technologically advanced world of mining, when other countries possess higher grade mineral ores than Zimbabwe? You must understand that Zimbabwe is a very small player in the world of mining; therefore our cost curve needs to be properly managed for our industry to remain competitive on the world market. We also need to appreciate that the world is changing fast in all aspects, and we must keep pace with that rapid change if we are to be recognized as a significant player.

With respect to human-resource development, Zimbabwe has seen a number of indigenous Zimbabweans assuming senior managerial positions in the mining industry in the last seventeen years. Some large mining companies have taken deliberate steps to develop most of their management resources in-house, with reasonable success. I personally applaud this approach and hope that it continues. Several mining companies have also shown deliberate reluctance to spend money developing their senior-level employees to take on higher responsibilities. What we have seen frequently in those companies is a desire to attract competent, well-developed and skilled individuals by offering very attractive salary and benefits packages, some of which are not necessarily commensurate with positions' responsibilities or management empowerment. This is not healthy for the mining industry or for the people concerned, as they will not have potential for growth in management in such organizations. I do not accept the deliberate overrating of positions, as it will prove detrimental to those individuals in the long run.

I feel downhearted each time I listen to top managers talk about solving a skills shortage in their companies by bringing in such skills from outside. What I often notice is that such managers will end up developing a highly demotivated workforce which sees no meaningful future for themselves in the organization. Such managers, in my view, fail to manage change because, unfortunately, their approach is maintenance management. I keep stressing that management is about change and a visionary approach to future organizational strategies. This approach is more pertinent for mining in Zimbabwe in the face of stiff competition from larger and more technologically advanced countries.

Zimbabwe's mining industry comprises some of the largest companies in the country. The country is going through various economic and institutional changes. It is natural to expect that disproportionate attention be paid to the mining industry, especially in the current debate on indigenous economic empowerment. My honest advice to the mining industry is to avoid overreacting to events. Be ahead of the debate by accepting the need for your company to participate in empowerment and to implement it rationally and effectively, for the benefit of your company and the country. You must not see it as an exogenously imposed requirement. Rather, you need to take ownership of it and seek to implement it at your company's own pace, with your own resources, if possible. Change process is all around in the Zimbabwean environment in which you are operating your business. You must therefore take appropriate steps to learn how to manage that change, before the change manages you and you are forced to react to it. The days when few large companies had exclusive rights to mining claim throughout the country are over, and such exclusivity can no longer be tolerated in light of the changing circumstances in the country. I can tell you that there is already a strong drive for small mining operators to become involved in the mining sector. This change must be managed effectively if the desired results are to be achieved, by ensuring that small mining operators are permitted to operate effectively in the mining industry

The art of managing change requires that if you as managers uphold the universal motherhood statement, "People are our most important assets," then you should indeed have a clear understanding of what kind of assets you want to acquire, at what cost and why. You should develop your human resources to ensure continued efficiency in your organization. You should develop these resources to ensure their effective progression into senior positions. This calls for total commitment from top management to precise strategic planning, visionary leadership with tangible, clear objectives for where your company is going, and effective communication of that vision down the organizational chain. This is the sum of management's ability to manage change in the mining industry in Zimbabwe.

On 27 October 1988, I officially opened the Anglo American Personnel Managers Conference in Harare, Zimbabwe, with the following address. I began by stressing that Anglo top management attach great importance to these conferences. I believe that they are an essential link that facilitates exchange of operating experiences, and they provide a forum for the open discussion of common issues and problems, allowing joint problem-solving approaches to be examined and tested for effective application to a variety of issues facing managers in a very trying environment.

I strongly believe that the degree to which organizations can achieve success in human-resource management will depend to a very large extent on the calibre, innovativeness, experience, ability and skilfulness of human-resource managers. If this is true, then human-resource managers must be well-informed about trends in human-resource development and shortcomings. They must possess skills to enable them to appropriately advise senior management concerning all aspects of employees' roles, welfare and skills development.

Human-resource management in modern societies (developed or developing) is becoming a very sophisticated science. Humans are becoming more complex. The tools and technology we use to achieve our desired results are also becoming more complex. You will notice that I have deliberately avoided the use of the term "personnel manager" and have instead preferred the term "human-resource manager." This is because I honestly do not believe that you should see yourselves purely as systems-maintenance men and women. You must instead see yourselves as adaptive and innovative managers, capable of transforming your organizations so that they can keep pace with the ever-changing environment in which they operate and can accept and manage change.

I must draw your attention to the Labour Relations Act in Zimbabwe, which, despite its flaws, is a test case of how human-resource managers like yourselves will be able to condition your organizations to manage changing circumstances.

It is often very easy to prescribe simplistic solutions to human-relations problems that arise in work situations. Some managers have a tendency to rush to conclusions, believing that they know the cause of a particular problem. The human-resource manager should assist the entire management structure in developing and cultivating a management culture that values effective problem-solving techniques, which require the identification of the real problem first before solutions are prescribed.

Whether you are dealing with simple grievance procedures, disciplinary cases or motivational problems, you need to be satisfied that effective problem-solving techniques have been applied. I merely want to provoke your thoughts on effective processes for decision making and problem solving with the hope that you might find answers to the question, "How can we be effective human-resource managers?"

Implementing total quality management also means preventing errors instead of merely correcting them. The development of quality is primarily a matter of attitude of each individual in each team and the company as a whole. For our industries to survive and grow in the changing environment of Southern Africa, the production of quality products and services has to be our first priority. To survive, Zimbabwean companies must emulate successful companies in Asia, Europe and America. They must set new standards of excellence for themselves. Doing so will demand disciplined leadership and vision, as well as changes in management style and behaviour in day-to-day operations and performance.

The Institute of Personnel Management in South Africa invited me to give a keynote address at their annual convention, held at Pilanesburg Convention Centre, Sun City, South Africa, on 28 September 1987. My address was titled "Problems and Solutions for Management in a Multicultural Society."

I began by highlighting that a lot has been said or written by human-resource-management scientists, academics and practitioners concerning the need for businesses to incorporate human-resource-management strategies in their overall corporate plans. Few organizations, both in developed and developing societies, have made significant achievements in this respect. One school of thought might blame top management for failing to recognize the importance of human-resource management in the company's decision-making process. Another school of thought might believe that the human-resource specialist in an organization is to blame for failing to persuade top management to acknowledge the importance of human-resource management in the company's strategic management plans. My strong belief is that both levels of management have a responsibility to ensure that human-resource-management strategies are incorporated in the company's overall plan if top management officials are to avoid or minimize the tendency to react to human-resource problems when they occur in the organization, rather than address them before they happen.

I tend to use the word "culture" in a restricted sense, to mean the collective programming of the mind that influences factors such as social, political and economic constraints or opportunities and the way individuals interpret the meaning of symbols. In South Africa, I believe managers face one of the most demanding environments in the world. To cope with any meaningful social and political change in this environment, managers and professionals must acquire skills well beyond those of basic management. You must have a reasonable understanding and appreciation of politics because your business-management decisions and strategies necessarily reflect an accommodation of political action in your work environment. You have to appreciate that your workers are also part of the political process and are likely to perceive their social and economic disadvantages as a consequence of the current political system. They are therefore likely to articulate their political demands through social and economic groups such as trade unions and workers' committees. The result is likely to be industrial unrest.

I noticed that some of the labour movements in South Africa have developed a reasonably high degree of effectiveness, even by world standards. They are now being recognized as legitimate representatives of workers in South Africa. The National Union of Mine Workers, for example, has become quite powerful, and its recent strike clearly demonstrates that point. Management in industries such as the mining industry needs to understand that a lot of demands and grievances workers raise reflect broader issues affecting them than mere job-related problems. It would be naïve for management to believe that if, for example, existing hostels for workers were improved, then workers would become happy. Regrettably, that would not be so. The long-term solution would certainly be management's initiative to remove social and cultural problems associated with denying a person the right to raise a family as a cohesive social unit living under one roof. Management needs to view a worker, regardless of rank, status or race, as a complete human being with set beliefs about and attitudes towards the legitimacy of systems of authority. Workers need self-actualization, and they have some perception of how they ought to play their roles as workers, parents and members of an economic class or political organization. Management should therefore avoid the danger of overemphasizing workers' allegiance to their employers and instead appreciate the diverse roles workers are expected to play in the broader community.

I wish to strongly stress that it is not enough for management to be satisfied with mere optimism for establishing non-racial opportunities in the workplace. There must be concrete evidence of developments towards those desires. As managers, are you able to say to what extent your own organization has developed strategies to hire, train, develop and promote your workers, through a well-defined career path, to fill various positions on the basis of merit rather than racial consideration? This is one of the pertinent questions that need to be addressed in your organizations. It seems to me that if large-scale social, economic and management problems are to be resolved effectively in South Africa, then management must recognize the need to resolve these problems on a small scale first. Individual companies must take the initiative and must have commitment in order to change the status quo.

While it is important that top management accepts changes to hiring and promoting workers in an organization, it is even more important that line managers, who must implement such policy changes, accept the framework of the new policy direction. Without line managers' acceptance, no effective change will take place. Management should not fear White-displacement backlash if the process of change is well planned and continued economic expansion is assured. It should be realized, however, that middle managers are the most threatened by any change to the status quo. There is, therefore, a need to reassure them that their positions will not necessarily be threatened. That will encourage them to identify Black workers capable of being developed for high management positions.

I certainly believe that top management has to be courageous enough not to permit the continuation of the belief that non-Whites in South

Africa are capable only of rising to certain levels in an organization. Management ought to reject such generalizations. Non-White workers have not been given sufficient opportunity and time to gain the necessary skills and experience on the job as have been deliberately given to their White counterparts. Management must therefore take the lead in pushing for development of all employees to eliminate racial disparities in hiring, training, development and promotion. This is one way of reducing the potential for conflict inherent in business management in South Africa today.

Before independence in Zimbabwe, we never had businesses managed by people with a progressive orientation to positive change and for the business community to become leaders in initiating that change. Instead, our top management failed to anticipate and prepare for change, and their organizations were eventually caught with untrained, inexperienced non-Whites who were then forced to assume positions of responsibility. These promotions of untrained and inexperienced workers to positions beyond their level of competence threw some companies into maladministration and poor organizational performance. I sincerely hope that top managers in South Africa will avoid being bedevilled with problems associated with appointments made for window dressing. You must adopt effective human-resource-management strategies for developing adequate numbers of suitably trained and experienced non-White workers to assume positions of responsibility in the future. Avoid regretting missed opportunities and being like many Zimbabwean business executives these days who say, "If only we had started our training and development programs twenty years ago."

I sincerely hope that I am not creating a wrong impression in your minds by my remarks. I am not advocating a policy of discrimination in favour of non-Whites in your hiring and promotion practices in South Africa. What I am suggesting is that the way out is to begin now, and continue at your own pace, by establishing training and staff-development programs in your companies that will prepare all workers to assume positions of responsibility in the near future. I know that this requires effort by human-resource-management specialists to convince top management, as well as line management, of the necessity and appropriateness of anticipating and preparing for change now.

Shortly after independence, Zimbabwe experienced a mass exodus of skilled and experienced White people. They either would not accept the changed political situation or doubted the future economic viability of the country. At that time, the country faced the problem of having to place inexperienced and inadequately trained personnel in important positions, especially in government and parastatal business organizations, mainly through presidential directives. This was considered the only alternative to continued reliance on expatriate human resources at a time when the two races in the country were highly suspicious of each other's intentions. It is generally accepted that positive results were achieved in such a short time. However, it is also true that a number of instances of maladministration were experienced. This could have been avoided, as I have stated before, if sufficient planning had been implemented to prepare for change before Zimbabwe achieved its independence.

In South Africa, I believe that mass exodus of Whites may not happen soon after democratic process replaces apartheid. The big question is, What will happen to non-White South Africans, who all along have been kept out of proper management systems because of apartheid rules of employment? Could they honestly believe that they would significantly change, after their continued exclusion from training and development programs, when they assumed positions of responsibility after apartheid? I believe not. The answer lies in top management, including line managers, in South Africa preparing non-White workers with skills and experience to perform well and to earn equal pay and providing them competitive opportunities to take on responsible positions, regardless of their race.

Sociologists have often stated that the biggest problem in human relationships is ensuring that one's intentions, beliefs, social mores and behaviour patterns are appropriately interpreted and clearly understood by the other party in the dialogue.

Often, management communication systems place emphasis on downward communication to ensure that management policies are understood and implemented properly. There is no deliberate plan to facilitate upward communication, whereby workers can initiate ideas about their work situation and communicate them up to management with the possibility that management might be receptive to such ideas. Sadly, workers are developed only to take orders and are unable to initiate new ideas to improve their performance. If they get promoted to higher-level positions, they find it difficult to perform effectively because all they know is how to carry out orders. You will be surprised to note that such a situation can be even more difficult for non-White employees whose cultural backgrounds force them to adhere to certain normative behaviour patterns based on age or sex.

In Zimbabwe, a number of programs for enhancing communication between employees and management have been developed. Some of these programs have the aim of establishing a workplace environment in which employees feel a sense of belonging to the company by encouraging regular and formally structured dialogue between workers and management.

The annual employee performance appraisal, in which the worker and manager discuss the employee's problems and successes and draw up the employee's future career development, is clearly accepted as a useful development and communication tool. The employee has a formal forum in which to communicate upwards, providing feedback to the immediate supervisor through an independent panel of management officials. Problems of expectations for the employee's career are identified early, and efforts to accommodate these expectations are communicated to the employee as well. Negative performance tendencies likely to delay fulfillment of the employee's expectations are also highlighted. This approach has seen extremely positive results, and I would certainly urge more large and small companies and organizations in South Africa to adopt a similar program.

In every organization in Zimbabwe, workers' committees and work councils have been set up through legislation. These committees and councils are democratically elected by workers to represent workers. Works councils, comprising workers' representatives elected by workers and management, meet regularly to discuss and solve a variety of problems at the workplace concerning production, conditions of employment, morale, and so on. As I have stated earlier, such communication programs help the workforce to feel that they are a strong part of the organization. This is a remarkable achievement towards industrial peace and harmony.

One point regarding the problem of handling change in South Africa seems certain: You as managers must first accept that your workers, or potential workers, regardless of their race, cultural background or position in the organization, are a whole human beings with beliefs about and attitudes towards the legitimacy of authority systems in your society. Values and rules imposed by apartheid policy in South Africa will come to an end. However, both White and non-White people must be prepared to come together to formulate management programs that will be realistic and meaningful to your organizations' effective operation in the future.

The *Weekly Mail* in South Africa reported positively on my address in which I further stressed my belief that it was essential for South African managers to begin the dialogue of change now, before the change is forced on them. If business managers initiate change processes by establishing training and staff-development programs that prepare their workers to assume responsible positions in the future, then they will not have to wait for government to remove apartheid laws first.

In my address and official opening of the second gold mine in Zimbabwe by Anglo American in 14 months, I again stressed that we were witnessing a clear demonstration of Anglo Group's financial and technical capacity to deploy its human resources' technical and managerial expertise to carry out grassroots exploration and to move quickly from exploration to new mining operations. This was a clear demonstration of the establishment of opportunities for job creation and foreign-currency earnings in Zimbabwe.

When I further addressed and officially opened the expansion of Portland's Colleen Bawn Cement Plant in Matabeleland, Zimbabwe, on 21 August 1998, I highlighted the favourable investment climate in Zimbabwe, brought about by the government's policy of liberalizing the economy in the early 1990s. This liberalization of the economy greatly encouraged investor confidence, which was critical to the success of capital intensiveness, and as a result, we would be able to increase Portland's cement production to a million tonnes a year. I also stressed that this would also mean increased road construction, property construction and increased export earnings that would benefit not only Anglo and other investors but also Zimbabwe in the form of increased tax revenue and increased job opportunities for Zimbabweans.

The keynote address I delivered at Sun City, South Africa, on 28 September 1987 generated wide publicity in South African print and television media. As a result, I was invited by several companies and organizations in South Africa to meet with or address issues raised by top management and boards of directors, and I accepted some of these invitations. In Durban, for example, I addressed top management and directors of Van Den Berg and Jurgens Private Limited, Unilever Group, on 9 November 1987.

I decided to provoke their thoughts on the problem of attitudes in human-resource management. I believed this to be critical, as all needed to appreciate the diverse cultural, social, economic and political backgrounds of members of all organizations in South Africa. I emphasized, therefore, that it was necessary for prudent managers to incorporate appropriate human-resource-management techniques into their strategic plans to maximize the use of the physical resources available to the organisation. I honestly believe that managers the world over must appreciate that they now must manage employees with different values and beliefs, priorities and work attitudes. Managers should therefore show an interest in finding out why their employees' belief systems are what they are.

The invasion of politics into business organizations is also increasingly affecting the life of a manager, and internal politics are also becoming a key part of everyday management life. I sincerely believe that managers and team leaders must be able to articulate the goals of their organizations in a clear manner that excites workers with different value systems. A key reason that is often proposed for management success in Japan is Japanese managers' ability to foster team spirit through symbolic events and activities that assist workers in considering and appreciating corporate needs and goals in addition to their own. It is important, therefore, for a manager to realize that the levels of effective communications and good leadership are under his control.

Today's managers are constantly faced with making decisions they have never before made, with having to create excellence in difficult business productions, and with having to build new strategies to resolve ever more complex organizational problems. Given all these circumstances, the most difficult problems for a manager are people problems, yet people are also the most valuable assets for an organization. What this suggests then is that management must intensify the search for a formula for human-resource development which will give an organization and all its workers the appropriate attitudes and beliefs to effectively realize organizational objectives while permitting self-actualization for workers.

I emphasize again, that managers must be equipped with the skills to manage change. The current environment in South Africa demands managers and professionals with skills that go well beyond those for basic management. Management may feel that significant progress has been made towards Black advancement while Black workers feel that very little progress has been made in this respect. Management's measurements of progress are often considered unrealistic by workers. In Zimbabwe, the most frequent complaint reported since independence has been that companies were slow or unwilling to appoint Blacks to effective managerial positions and that when such appointments were made, management responsibilities were watered down to a point where Black managers could not make meaningful or effective decisions. This is a practical problem. It certainly highlights the fact that top managers failed to plan management development strategically in preparation for change. Therefore, the appointment of Blacks to management positions were often merely window dressing, with their managerial responsibilities watered down because they were not ready to assume effective decision-making positions. The blame here lies totally on top managers within such a company for failing to develop and prepare Black workers to assume effective management roles.

The general attitude of Blacks in Zimbabwe to this problem was twofold. First, they resented being penalized for White managers' inability and unwillingness to anticipate change and to prepare for it before independence by training and developing Blacks and allowing them to gain experience. Second, Blacks sincerely believed that White managers used Blacks' lack of experience as an excuse to perpetuate the long-held stereotype that Blacks were incapable of assuming senior management positions.

As I see it, organizations in South Africa, particularly the Unilever Group, the problem I have described awaits you if you maintain the status quo as dictated by apartheid. You now have an opportunity to avoid making some of the mistakes Zimbabwe made before independence and learn that Zimbabwe's problems will be short-lived because our educational system for Blacks and Whites was the same, unlike your educational system here under apartheid. My sincere wish is that you adopt a progressive stance to train, develop and promote your Black workers to some relatively senor positions now to allow them to gain the necessary experience to do a good job in the future, when apartheid is removed.

In all this, deliberate planning which assumes that change is certainly coming within the wider social system in South Africa is a necessary condition for peaceful relations in the workplace in the future. The degree to which organizations communicate these plans effectively with the workforce is likely to distinguish progressive organizations, which are likely to have continued harmonious industrial relations and high commitment to the organisation, from those bedevilled by recurring industrial strife in the long run. There are, however, several pertinent questions management must address in order to train, develop and promote Blacks to senior positions. Middle managers are the ones who will ultimately be responsible for the implementing of these plans, and most, if not all, of those currently holding these positions are White. To what extent can they be reassured that their own positions are not threatened by the development of Black potential managers? Will there be enough senior positions available to promote Blacks into them without affecting White middle managers? Is there sufficient room for horizontal growth in the organization to absorb newly developed Blacks, or is natural attrition sufficient to absorb those Black workers? These and many other questions need to be addressed if resistance to change by White middle managers is to be avoided.

Training and development of Blacks should not happen at the expense of junior White employees, who also expect to be developed for promotion to senior positions. If they perceive their chances of upward promotion are threatened by the development of Blacks, you can be sure of severe resistance by Whites to any plans for change.

In Zimbabwe, many Whites' attitudes and beliefs have dramatically changed since independence. I can only assume that most of them have developed comfortable and close relations and communication with Blacks, helping them to see reason to make positive contributions to progress in the changed environment. Blacks have also achieved attitudinal transformations in order to earn the respect and recognition of Whites and to gain sympathy for their plight.

What I have been trying to persuade you to accept is that the problem of attitudes is not just a question of White and Black workers, especially during periods when society as a whole is undergoing change. It is a question of perceived advantages or disadvantages associated with one's membership to a particular social, economic or political grouping in society as whole. Therefore, the extent to which anyone from any group accepts or resists change depends on their perception of what they will lose or gain from accepting change.

The current South African situation is totally different from the Zimbabwean situation before independence. Disparities in educational systems in South Africa are regrettable. These institutionalized educational disparities means that Blacks require longer to train and develop the skills for them to compete on an equal footing with whites for appointments to senior positions. I sincerely believe that the immediate and long-term solution to human-resource problems in formal organizations in South Africa is continued maintenance of industrial peace and a high level of production. This requires that managers prioritize creating an environment in which they can effectively manage change. They need to instill a common sense of belonging in employees of all races and a belief that management at all levels has a commitment to positive change in the company.

I made an interesting address to the Chamber of Zimbabwe Industries on 16 June 1994 called "Business Linkages." In it, I presented my strong belief that small organizations in Zimbabwe have a particular role to play in generating economic growth and employment in our country.

I began by highlighting some research conducted by Newcastle University in the United Kingdom for the Department of Employment. This showed that between 1982 and 1991, firms with fewer than 20 employees created 2.5 million net jobs and that their larger counterparts actually shed a quarter of a million jobs within the same period. Statistics from mature (developed) economies also demonstrated that employment in small firms grew dramatically between 1979 and 1991. However, despite this level of growth, there has been clear evidence of dissatisfaction with the financing available to small firms. This brings me to our own interest in Zimbabwe, as we try to establish links between large companies and emerging small firms. Small firms in developing countries face the same financing problems as small firms in developed countries: financial institutions are reluctant to lend money to firms without adequate security.

In order to promote the whole concept of business linkages, Anglo American Corporation Zimbabwe established a venture capital company, Hawk Ventures Limited, in 1991. Like all venture capital companies, Hawk's main objective was to provide initial financial support for viable projects that promoters presented to the company. Of course, this support would only be provided following rigorous project evaluation to determine that satisfactory compliance with a set of guidelines and conditions established by Hawk Ventures had been met.

Anglo has used Hawk Ventures as a vehicle to utilize shareholders' funds to promote entrepreneurial initiatives in Zimbabwe. At Hawk, we had a deliberate policy to support any viable stipulated project costing, favouring of projects with strong export potential.

It seems to me that effective linkages between small businesses and large companies or financial institutions require that those who have finances understand the *sui generis* needs of small-business customers. Small businesses, on their part, must equally understand the requirements of financing organizations. Hawk Ventures initially invested millions of dollars in a variety of projects which seemed viable at the time of project appraisal. In addition, Hawk gave millions as guarantees in support of loan applications to banks to assist in raising additional working capital for those projects.

The biggest flaw in arranging financing for small businesses, in my view, was the lack of insistence on appropriate training and development of promoters of projects as a precondition for project approval. Very often there is an assumption that because the promoter brings in a viable project, that promoter has the ability to manage it successfully. This is wrong. Hawk Ventures discovered that good projects collapsed because of lack of management ability, lack of appropriate financial background or lack of marketing ability. I sincerely believe that linkages between small businesses and large companies or financing institutions should be promoted in Zimbabwe, but I also believe that some fundamental questions must first be addressed:

- How do we ensure that promoters of projects to be financed have been adequately exposed to the appropriate business culture?

- How do we ensure that promoters of projects appreciate the need for some minimum training before embarking on the project?

- Should the large organizations identify potential entrepreneurs among their own employees and encourage them to undertake projects with the organization's financial, technical and management support for a stipulated time?

- Should the Zimbabwean government not have a deliberate policy to encourage development of small formal businesses and their linkages with large business organizations, and also introduce certain tax holidays and waivers of import duties and taxes to encourage such ventures?

- Do we believe that the emergence of small-business initiatives could be effective in times of structural economic adjustment, at times of high inflation and high interest rates?

At the end of the day, I regret the us-versus-them perceptions of big and small businesses. We are all one, I believe, and all of us must be given every opportunity to grow, because by doing so, we will all provide jobs, foreign currency and economic expansion in the country as a whole.

On 18 July 1995, I was appointed Chairman of Astra Corporation Group while I was still an Anglo executive, Director of the Reserve Bank of Zimbabwe, and director of several companies in Zimbabwe. In my official opening speech of Astra Paints' new administration building in Harare, Zimbabwe, on 27 January 1999, I highlighted our board's confidence in the future of the Astra Group in Zimbabwe. Within the Astra Group, we had always taken pride in marshalling our resources with a view to improving, modernizing and expanding our facilities to position our business competitively. Over the past four years, we had completed a number of significant projects in our business operations that enhanced our competitive position. At Zemco, for example, we completed a major project that more than doubled our workshop area, re-equipped the transmission service bay, and installed a hydraulic cylinder bay, oil analysis laboratory, and other facilities. We also moved our Henry Dunn Steel and Engineering Equipment operations in Harare to much larger premises. We further installed new machinery and modernized the heavy-transport fleet.

In addition to these developments, we more than doubled the factory and office space at Paprika Zimbabwe by installing more efficient milling-plant and paprika-handling equipment. In 1997, we put up our own double-story building in Beitbridge, providing Expeditors' branch there with spacious, air-conditioned office accommodation and a secure warehouse for clients' goods in transit. In 1995, the Cairns subsidiary acquired the Liebigs Canning business in Mutare, Zimbabwe. This helped Cairns to develop economies of scale, thereby enhancing the company's competitiveness.

All these developments within the Astra Group made me believe that the Group had performed extremely well in the harsh economic environment and that it had consolidated its business interests. I strongly believed then that the Group must therefore be looking at expanding and refocusing on core business activities, namely, earth moving, paints and foods. The Astra Group had been at the heart of Zimbabwean economic development for many years. The food and wine businesses of Cairns helped to develop agriculture by providing important markets for farmers in Zimbabwe. Astra's agricultural and earth-moving businesses contributed for many years to the development of Zimbabwe. Farmec supplied tractors and agricultural equipment, and the Caterpillar franchise helped build roads, bridges and dams in Zimbabwe. All these activities moved the Zimbabwean economy in the right direction.

On 9 February 2000, I had the greatest privilege to list Astra Limited on the Zimbabwe Stock Exchange. I emphasized in my speech this listing had been our goal for many years. We had always believed that it would widen ownership of Astra and thus position and equip the Group for further growth.

I was subsequently very pleased that Astra achieved combined turnover of several billions of dollars, a market capitalization of billions of dollars, and it traded as one of the top 15 companies on the Zimbabwe Stock Exchange.

Even though I continued as Chairman of Astra Limited, we had a very strong desire to demerge the Group into three public quoted companies on the Stock Exchange, whereby each company would continue to possess its subsidiary companies. This enabled me to develop prospective top managers and to appoint boards of directors for each company. For some time after the establishment of these three company boards, I remained chairman of each one of them. I wanted to feel satisfied that these three companies continued to perform competitively. I was extremely pleased that the three companies did perform well. Share prices were constantly rising, profits were also rising and shareholders' dividend payments were pleasing.

All these positive business results encouraged me to appoint three new chairmen to take over from me. Not only that but training and development of appropriate employees had also been going on to ensure that these three companies would have well-developed individuals ready to assume senior management positions and responsibilities in the future. This is what I emphasized in all my speeches in Zimbabwe and South Africa: In order to plan for managing change in your company or organization, you must prepare and develop human resources to be ready to manage change. I remained happy with my appointments of chairmen and managing directors of the three companies. They gave me full confidence of continued good performance into the future. I was therefore comfortable retiring from being chairman of these companies.

My visit to some training institutions in South Africa after attending a management seminar there, I certainly concluded that Anglo American Corporation Zimbabwe needed to consider the possibility of establishing a similar training and development centre or institution in our country. My view was that such an institution or centre would be able to extend its training and development programs to other organizations in Zimbabwe. When I returned to Zimbabwe, I raised this issue with the Chairman of

Anglo, and he asked me to raise the issue at our daily executive meeting. When I did so, my colleagues did not believe that Anglo should spend millions of dollars to set up such an institution to help organizations outside Anglo Group. Since the Chairman supported my idea, he then privately asked me to proceed in establishing this institution without presenting further reports or raising further discussions on the issue at our daily executive meetings. I then proceeded accordingly, and I regularly briefed him on my progress.

I managed to purchase two property stands on the outskirt of the Harare city centre. I engaged an architectural firm to provide me with plans for the structure of the buildings as I had described them. Having completed their work and presented it to me, I then told them that I wanted all the buildings in the first stand, for management training and development, to have grass-thatched roofs and walls of unplastered brown bricks. I hoped that we would afterwards develop the second stand to cater to technical training and development. Unfortunately, I still haven't managed to develop this second stand to this day.

When construction of the management training and development stand was well advanced, I then raised the issue at our daily executive meeting and requested that my colleagues visit the premises, which we decided to call St. Lucia Park. When the Chairman and all my Anglo Executive colleagues came to St. Lucia Park, they were amazed by the development that had taken place. They were very pleased, and they expressed the hope that the institution would achieve its goals. I thanked them all for that.

On 28 June 1991, I addressed the official opening of St. Lucia Park, which was to be operated by a company called Organizational Training and Development (OTD), a company formed in 1988 for which I served as chairman.

In my address, I pointed out that the premises comprised three professionally designed training rooms, 7 syndicate rooms, a central refreshment area, 26 single bedrooms and 4 double bedrooms all with en suite bathrooms, a dining room designed to seat 56 people, and a lounge. The park also included a block of offices for all trainers, managers and general administration. I also indicated that our catering department was headed by a professional hotelier and that it would provide around-the-clock service to our students, clients and staff.

I pointed out that it took me nine months to obtain approval from the Harare City Council to construct the buildings. These were the first public buildings in the capital city of Zimbabwe to all have grass-thatched roofs. I finally persuaded the City Council to approve the construction by stressing that the ceilings in all buildings would be constructed of concrete to minimize fire hazards.

Some progress was made in developing clientele for OTD. More than 120 non-Anglo clients in Zimbabwe were developed from the private and public sectors as well as from donor aid organizations. Several regional clients were also developed, especially from Angola and Mozambique. Inquiries were also received from Kenya, Malawi, Zambia and Botswana that are being followed up with a view to offering these potential clients relevant existing programs or tailoring our programs for their local human-resource training and development needs.

As a unique training institution, OTD was in a position to access proven training packages from reputable international human-resource development organizations. For example, I invited three professors of business from Harvard University in the United States, whom I had met in South Africa while attending a management seminar, to come to OTD to present their programs to me and to the OTD chief executive. They did this over four days. I accepted their programs, and we then dovetailed them with Anglo's existing human-resource training and development programs. We developed and continued to develop a wide range of training programs appropriate for all levels of management personnel in an organization.

The ultimate success of Zimbabwe's Economic Structural Adjustment Programme depends not only on the availability of financial resources but, to a very large extent, it also depends on the effectiveness of the country's human resources. OTD hoped to play its role in developing and equipping human resources at all levels in an organization so that they might contribute efficiently and effectively to the success of the company. We were extremely pleased by several international organizations that expressed interest in using OTD in their various programs for Zimbabwe and its neighbouring countries.

My total commitment to and involvement in the establishment of OTD at St. Lucia Park and its collaboration with a number of human-resource training and development programs from international institutions and managers in important positions in several organizations have given me absolute satisfaction in my lifetime of achievements.

⇢ EIGHT ⇠

Establishment of Export Processing Zones in Zimbabwe

The Zimbabwean government appreciated the significant economic progress of many countries that had established export processing zones (EPZs) in their environments. At that time, countries such as Ireland and Malaysia clearly demonstrated how to use EPZs to profitably improve their business activities and economies.

The Zimbabwean Parliament passed the Export Processing Zones Authority Act, establishing a parastatal organization in the country that introduced the establishment of business operations that would enjoy tax exemptions . On 7 March 1996, Zimbabwe's Minister of Industry and Commerce, Dr. H. M. Murerwa, appointed me Chairman of Export Processing Zones Authority, with the approval of the President.

I made several addresses at many meetings of various organizations in Zimbabwe to the new concept of EPZs in Zimbabwe to the attention of business communities. I highlighted the fact that some countries in Africa, such as Kenya, had already implemented this concept in their drive to improve their economic performance.

On 5 July 1996, I addressed the Ninth Annual General Meeting of the Horticultural Promotion Council in Zimbabwe. I stressed how desirable the EPZ concept would have been for Zimbabwe if the government had implemented it before the Economic Structural Adjustment Programme (ESAP). The country would have seen much economic benefit had it implemented the EPZ, say, six years before it introduced the ESAP. However, I maintained that it was better to implement this concept late than to never have implemented it at all.

The main role of EPZs was to permit export-oriented industrial activities, whether they be manufacturing processes, assembly of goods, or services for exporting such goods. I emphasized that EPZs implied geographical demarcations of areas within which specific sets of competitive incentives would be applied to motivate would-be investors. I was cognizant of the delay in Zimbabwe's establishing EPZs, and I stressed that the Export Processing Zones Authority board of directors, would move rather quickly to establish this program. We had already interviewed and appointed a managing director of the EPZ, and I was quite pleased with the speed with which we established the EPZ afterward.

I discussed the functions of the EPZ empowered by the EPZ Act passed by Parliament. These functions were to administer, control, manage and regulate activities and performance of all export processing zones; to permit customs offices to be established in any such zone; to grant licences for investment in these zones; and to grant permits to developers of EPZ industrial parks.

In my business management experience, I had not had direct exposure to the activities of EPZs. Nevertheless, I studied EPZ programs in other countries and found that many had achieved great economic successes thanks to their EPZs. I subsequently conducted discussions with Irish and Malaysian managers and consultants who had vast experience in establishing EPZ programs in their countries. I also wished to attach some of Zimbabwe's managers to these countries to gain hands-on experience with EPZ operations. I organized a trip to Malaysia for my entire board of directors to also give them practical exposure to the actual operations of EPZ projects there.

In my address at the Employers' Confederation of Zimbabwe (EMCOZ) Seminar on Investment and Employment Creation, on 21 August 1996, I explained that the incentives offered by the EPZ Authority were equally available to domestic and foreign companies and to individual investors. I emphasized that Zimbabwe would benefit from the success of the EPZ initiative through the creation of more jobs, the injection of new investment capital, increased exports, technology transfer and local business linkages.

I also provided details of further EPZ incentives:

- five-year tax holiday
- 15 percent corporate tax after the five-year holiday
- exemption from duties for goods imported into EPZs
- exemption from capital gains tax; exemption from withholding taxes on interest paid, fees, remittances and royalties for a person operating in an EPZ
- exemption from fringe benefits tax for employees of EPZ companies
- exemption from sales tax on goods and services
- permission for foreign companies to borrow locally.

I provided further details about the criteria for evaluating projects for EPZ, especially the stipulations that at least 80 percent of product sales must be for export and the need for significant new capital investment must be clearly demonstrated. These criteria would ensure that proposed projects created new jobs, enhanced technology transfer and allowed for additional production in the case of expansion.

I was pleased to note that the EPZ Authority was in a hurry to have investments flow into Zimbabwe. We therefore could not accept unnecessary delays in reviewing project applications. The EPZ Act authorized me as the Chairman of the EPZ Authority to sign all investment licences, developers' permits and EPZ licences to give investors the incentives already mentioned.

During my speech at the EPZ Conference on 28 October 1996, I emphasized that export-oriented activities in Zimbabwe would benefit from the country's rich resources, its relatively well-developed infrastructure and industrial support services, as well as its educated, disciplined, hard-working and competitive labour force. Therefore, Zimbabwe's EPZ Authority not only offered attractive incentives but also provided a stable and dynamic investment climate. The overall Zimbabwean investment environment offered investors the additional incentives of free remittance of dividends, free movement of investment capital, and complete ownership and control of their businesses.

I was featured in an interesting article titled "Has He Got Too Much on His Plate?", published in Zimbabwe's premier business magazine, *Mega Buck*, in August, 1996 and accompanied by my photograph. The article described my "hectic business life," detailing my involvement in all the companies and organizations for which I served as chairman or director and my own business investments, including in Expedition Airways, an airline of two airplanes that were to fly tourists to national parks in Zimbabwe, Mozambique and South Africa. I responded to the magazine with the following statement: "Indigenous people in Zimbabwe must know that despite difficulties they may face in business, they must go in to win not fail. There is a need to emphasize management and financial development programs. We must also know that we have to start simple and modest, until we have built a solid foundation."

What also interested me was my appointment by the Zimbabwe Conference Centre as chairman of the planning committee of the London Conference, which was to be held in London on 14 February 1997. The President of the Republic of Zimbabwe, Mr Robert Mugabe, accepted an invitation to provide the keynote address and to lead a delegation of more than 100 Zimbabwean business delegates to meet with British investors and banks. The London Conference took place after Zimbabwe's government had gone further in liberalizing the economy by making several important changes to the investment climate. Among these were an increase in the participation of foreign investors on the booming stock exchange, the relaxation of dual-listing rules of stock exchange by the Reserve Bank of Zimbabwe and the formation of our Export Processing Zones Authority.

As chairman of the planning committee, I strongly hoped that the conference would be more successful than previous conferences because a lot had happened in Zimbabwe since the last conference. I further explained that British businesspeople, already the largest investors in Zimbabwe, wanted clear answers on several government policies and the latest information on new opportunities in Zimbabwe. The conference in London turned out to be very successful in attracting more British investors to Zimbabwe.

In my first statement as Chairman of Zimbabwe's Export Processing Zone Authority, delivered on 30 June 1997, I pointed out that the EPZ board had experienced problems ranging from overlapping policies of the EPZ Act and other acts relevant to enterprise sectors that resulted in new investors being given attractive incentives not available to existing investors, giving those new investors a competitive advantage. Naturally, the existing investors were not happy.

I further expressed my pleasure that in a very short time since the establishment of EPZs in Zimbabwe, we managed to approve the investment operations of 87 companies and issue them with EPZ licences. The most impressive thing to me was that millions of dollars in export earnings had been generated and 7,271 new jobs had been created. This was commendable performance within such a short time.

I pointed out that because the EPZ Authority was a parastatal organization dealing with private-sector commercial activities, the biggest challenge was always ensuring that decisions were made quickly. Time cost a lot of money and often made the difference between winning or losing critical investment opportunities for the country. We needed to ensure that other government institutions involved in EPZ program understood and appreciated this.

The greatest satisfaction I obtained from my activity as EPZ Authority Chairman was in gaining our board's involvement in implementing the Rural Integrated Agro-Processing Exports program. I strongly believed that Zimbabwe's sustainable development would certainly lie in its ability to harness its abundant resources through a program such as this. Accordingly, the board agreed to engage a team of consultants to produce a detailed report and guidelines outlining ideal projects suitable for each province in Zimbabwe according to its resources and development that would facilitate the program. I then opened a three-day seminar at the Harare Conference Centre in Zimbabwe by presenting two volumes of the consultants' report and explaining that the EPZ Authority would be implementing this program throughout Zimbabwe. I was very pleased by the remarks of Mr. N. Shamuyarira, the Minister of Industry and

Commerce, who officially opened the seminar. He strongly praised my efforts and believed that the Authority would go further in developing Zimbabwe than the government could.

During my address at the Fourth African American Conference held on 25 July 1997 at the Harare Conference Centre in Zimbabwe, I outlined what I believed to be a strong, targeted investment drive in Southern Africa. I stated that perhaps part of the cause of lower than anticipated inflow of investments into our region could have been a lack of emphasis on targeting areas in our countries for capital inflow. I truly believed that this targeted approach to implementing the Rural Integrated Agro-Processing Exports program would certainly incentivize the inflow of capital into the region. I emphasized the value EPZ status would add to any investment project because of the EPZ Authority's full package of incentives. By offering these incentives, Zimbabwe would prove its comparative advantages, particularly for resource-based investment projects, because of the country's abundance of raw materials available at low cost.

On 28 January 1998 I was invited to address Southern Africa's Premier Summit on Infrastructure Development at VW Conference Centre in Midrand, Gauteng, South Africa. My address was titled "Experience Gathered in Setting Up Export Processing Zones in Zimbabwe."

I explained that the Zimbabwe Export Processing Zones Authority derived its powers from the Export Processing Zone Authority Act, which gave the Authority's board of directors wide-ranging powers for making policy decisions and monitoring the implementation of those decisions.

The biggest difficulty the Authority encountered as we implemented the EPZ program was that necessary changes to existing legislation, particularly to the Customs and Excise Act, had not been implemented.

Soon after we granted EPZ status to investment projects, thereby giving them exemptions from paying duties on imported capital and raw materials, customs officials still required that these projects pay duties.

Further, the EPZ Authority had assumed that customs officials understood how the EPZ program was intended to operate. That was too presumptuous of us. We should have spent more time educating customs officials about the program and ensuring their commitment to its successful implementation. Discussions between the EPZ Authority and the Ministry of Finance, which was responsible for Customs Department and the Ministry of Industry and Commerce, resulted in the issuance of statutory instruments to take care of the legislative overlaps and omissions, effectively resolving these problems.

The timing of the implementation of the EPZ program in Zimbabwe was rather unfortunate. The Zimbabwean government was facing financial difficulties which hindered any meaningful financial support for the program. This was not necessarily indicative of the government's lack of commitment but rather its genuine lack of financial resources to adequately fund the EPZ Authority. This severely constrained our efforts to effectively develop staff either through training and development programs or through exposure to successful EPZ programs elsewhere in the world.

EPZ programs in other countries, including Kenya, had been very fortunate that their governments freely gave them enough land on which to develop industrial parks and provided them with sufficient capital.

Existing investors in Zimbabwe made outcries that they could not enjoy the incentives EPZ programs offered to new investors for EPZ programs. Many of them pointed out that they exported more than 80 percent of their production, which was the threshold at which new EPZ investors would enjoy incentives. Existing investors further complained that new investors were given competitive advantages over them that might kill existing operations. I admitted that these were valid points. However, I emphasized that our EPZ program was intended to attract new investment to create additional production, additional employment and additional export earningsfor Zimbabwe, encouraging existing investors to expand their operations or implement new export-oriented projects.

The EPZ Authority had approved five industrial parks throughout Zimbabwe for EPZ activities, and the development of an industrial park at Beitbridge, on the border with South Africa, had begun. Several executives of various companies in South Africa had expressed their desire to be involved in the production of goods for export into South Africa at this industrial park, as our costs for these products would be cheaper than those of similar products produced in their country. I gave them a clear positive response. However, the development of these industrial parks tended to take longer than I had anticipated. Part of the problem was that the developers had to go through various stages for approval from local government authorities. The EPZ Authority had to continue working hard, together with developers, to obtain approval from these authorities as quickly as possible.

The EPZ Program impressed me very much, even though we experienced difficulties during its implementation. Looking back, I can see that the prices of commodities imported into Zimbabwe through EPZ areas were more competitive than those from existing operations outside EPZs. Not only that, but we created several thousand new jobs for Zimbabweans, maintained high inflows of new capital investment and achieved significant increases in production. All this made me happy.

In addition, tremendous downstream job creation that resulted from the establishment of the new investments for resource-based operations such as paprika processing. All the road shows we have conducted in Zimbabwe and overseas have helped to clarify the extent to which Zimbabwe's economy was open and market-based. I can therefore safely say that the launching of the EPZ program in Zimbabwe has had tremendous success in promoting the country as an appropriate destination for investment.

NINE

My Election as the First Black President of the Zimbabwe Chamber of Mines

The Zimbabwean media, including the *Financial Gazette*, reported strongly favourable on statement that I made following my election as President of the Chamber of Mines of Zimbabwe. In it, I promised to advocate for the mining sector's desperate need for foreign currency to facilitate the industry's efforts to procure mining equipment. Mining equipment for every mine was now obsolete and broken down, reducing production levels. I effectively pursued this issue during my term.

I was quite fascinated by newspapers' continued reports on my statements. This helped me to remind readers that the mining industry earned such a large proportion of foreign currency for Zimbabwe that it deserved high-priority status for the allocation of resources for it to expand operations, thus earning more foreign currency for Zimbabwe. At that time, the mining industry earned about 45 percent of the country's foreign currency and purchased about one-third of the electricity the country generated.

I sought an urgent solution between government and the mining sector to the problem of illegal gold-panning. I knew that the solution would be difficult to find because unemployment was forcing people to resort to this practice in alarmingly high numbers. Zimbabwe was losing about $50 million a year in gold revenues. I personally favoured the legalization of gold-panning in order to regulate it, as I was convinced that efforts to wipe out the practice by force would be futile, as was the case with the rhinoceros-poaching.

One of the biggest issues that I initially focused my attention on was safety in mining. I hoped to draw on international expertise to improve safety conditions in mining operations in Zimbabwe. Although our safety record was extremely good for a sector engaged in an admittedly dangerous activity, we did not have solutions to all our problems yet. In my role as President, I worked towards implementing tighter controls to prevent accidents in the industry as a whole.

My overall ambition was to be a very visible president. I needed to communicate better, to work more closely with relevant institutions, and to achieve more effective utilization of scarce resources. I intended to spend a lot of time on these tasks.

On 8 June 1990, while addressing an annual General Meeting of the Association of Mining Engineers of Zimbabwe in Harare, I applauded the launch of long-awaited investment guidelines and the government's proposal for a liberalization and economic structural-adjustment program that would bring about changes to the mining industry. I strongly urged the private sector to adopt a positive stand towards progressive government initiatives and to leave negativism and suspicion behind them. I could emphasize the mining industry's need to attract more foreign currency and supply of new equipment, in order to increase production and to reduce the shortage of skilled and experienced workers.

To remain competitive with mining organizations based elsewhere in the world, I strongly believed that Zimbabwe's mining industry had to increase its mineral exploration. The World Bank had carried out a study in 1987 showing a progressive decline in mineral exploration in sub-Saharan Africa. Zimbabwe allocated only 2.5 percent of gross revenues to exploration, which compared unfavourably with the huge amount of money other countries spent on exploration. In an address to the Economic Commission for Africa's workshop in Harare, I stressed that our mining industry needed to intensify its exploration in order to slow the decline in value production relative to our competitors elsewhere in the world.

In October 1990, I attended two investment conferences on the Zimbabwe mining sector in London and Sheffield, United Kingdom. News outlets in Zimbabwe widely reported my description of the conferences as "very encouraging." I indicated that both conferences managed to revitalize the waning interest in investment in Zimbabwe by British businesses. British investors were once again thinking about investing in Zimbabwe's mining industry. At these conferences, I did not wish to put emphasis on speeches but rather on dialogue, and I was forthright about that desire. I told British delegates of crucial changes taking place in Zimbabwe. I stressed to the top British business executives, bankers and investors attending the conferences that Zimbabwe's commitment to the economic structural-adjustment program was irreversible, and therefore the mining industry expected to further expand mining and production and to increase its human-resource development and experience.

In my message on Christmas 1990, I encouraged the mining industry to look back with satisfaction at its achievements as an exporter, and thus a major foreign-currency earner; as a supplier of raw materials for local industry; and as a significant contributor to employment and economic activity throughout Zimbabwe. I further highlighted that during the course of the year, I had made a number of visits to Japan, Canada and Europe to draw attention to Zimbabwe's mineral potential and attractive prospects in mining. In addition, I made several visits throughout our country to meet as many members of the mining industry as possible. I discussed problems on the ground, and I encouraged the industry to open up its communications and reach out to the wider Zimbabwean community so others would understand and appreciate the mining industry's contributions to the nation as a whole. I was pleased to say that this effort seemed to be bearing positive results.

I concluded my Christmas message by extending my best wishes to the entire mining community and to all those who serviced the industry for Christmas and a prosperous, accident-free New Year.

From 1 to 3 October 1990 I participated in the World Economic Forum in Geneva, Switzerland, as part of a strong private-sector delegation from Zimbabwe. During the discussion seminar on mining, I was asked to present a paper and to lead the discussion. The Zimbabwean delegation was very pleased with my presentation. In it, I pointed out that a clear and precise plan for the first phase of the Zimbabwean economic structural-adjustment program had been placed on the table. This program would show just how far Zimbabwe would go to meet the requirements of international investors in our country.

This presentation provoked a number of very good questions from delegates, especially from the United States. I responded to those questions well, I thought, and I actually enjoyed the discussion. Responses to Zimbabwe's new economic thrust and the interest shown by big financial investors at the World Economic Forum in Geneva had encouraged the Chamber of Mines to attend these two mining-investment conferences in London and Sheffield.

The Zimbabwe Chamber of Mines Annual General Meeting (AGM), on 30 May 1991, gave me the highest and most glorious joy of my service as President. I invited President Robert Mugabe to officially open the AGM, and he warmly accepted my invitation. That pleased me greatly because this was the first time the country's president had ever attended this meeting. What also pleased me was that many of the cabinet ministers we had invited also attended along with a huge crowd of delegates from the mining industry.

In his opening address at the AGM, President Mugabe stated that the mining sector was one of the pillars of Zimbabwe's economy, along with the agricultural and manufacturing sectors. He pointed out that mining itself was one of the oldest occupations and was inextricably bound with the development of our modern society. Over the ages, minerals had been extracted and processed by various methods to provide shelter, warmth, weapons, tools, adornments and wealth, to mention but a few uses. As communities developed, the processes to which minerals were subjected became more and more advanced. As a result, there are few products which do not owe their existence directly or indirectly to minerals. Minerals, if not a component of a product itself, are components of sophisticated machinery used to manufacture the component.

Mining in Zimbabwe has a rich history. Gold, copper and iron ore were mined centuries ago. In fact, very many of the mines that existed at the time of the AGM were on the sites of older mining locations. Most of the minerals and their concentrates processed in these modern mines were smelted and refined. Very few minerals were exported before this processing, but with few exceptions, they were thereafter exported in raw form as commodities and reimported in the form of manufactured goods. The importation of these manufactured goods implied the importation of the wages of those who made them together with other costs of production, marketing and transport. These processes contributed not only to job creation in other countries but also to their larger economic development. To become more industrialized and therefore add value to primary products for both domestic consumption and export was one of the greatest challenges facing developing countries, and one of the major thrusts of Zimbabwe's economic policies was to promote such industrial development.

There was, therefore, a great need for the mining and manufacturing sectors to work together to manufacture a wider range of finished goods. However, such development required the importation of resources we did not produce, including the raw materials and technology, especially sophisticated and expensive modern equipment. It is in the earning of foreign currency for the acquisition of such resources that the mining industry played a crucial role. In 1991, the mining industry earned almost 45 percent of Zimbabwe's foreign currency but used less than 10 percent of that currency, and therefore the downstream benefits of the availability of that foreign currency were considerable.

The President continued his speech by adding that government was aware of the constraints under which the mining sector operated. These included adverse international commodities prices, loss of skills and insufficient allocation of foreign currency for spare parts and equipment. Despite these problems, the mining industry had persevered and taken steps to keep mines operating, which was admirable. Government played its part in providing technical services to the industry through the Ministry of Mines in equally difficult circumstances. The export retention scheme was an effort to meet the constraints imposed by the shortage of foreign currency. The provision of US$75 million, negotiated through the Governor of the Bank of England, was intended to enable the mining industry to increase its production and thus exports.

Foreign investment in the mining sector was welcomed because exploration and the establishment of mines capable of achieving high levels of production required considerable financial and technological resources. The response of the international mining community to the opportunities for investment in Zimbabwe's mining sector was encouraging. However, this interest presented a challenge to domestic entrepreneurs, and steps needed to be taken to ensure that they were not left out. There was great potential for the further development of our mining resources, and Zimbabweans were encouraged to take the initiative to fully involve themselves in this development.

Encouraging the establishment of large mines did not imply that small and medium-sized mines had no place in the economy. Such mines, which accounted for some 15 percent of production, were generally locally owned. Small mines and co-operatives, in particular, were able to mine deposits that were not large enough to warrant extensive and costly infrastructure.

President Mugabe further indicated that by its very nature, mining is in conflict with the environment. However, he was pleased to note the concern of the Chamber of Mines for environmental issues and the response from mines to that concern. The competitions organized in conjunction with the Natural Resources Board and the general measures taken to promote awareness of the consequences of failure to repair the environment went a long way towards avoiding the environmental harm which would otherwise occur.

Zimbabwe's government was concerned with the problems arising from riverbed panning and illegal gold-dealing, and it sought a solution that did not remove the livelihood of alluvial gold miners operating legally, provided they used methods that would not damage river systems. At the same time, the government encouraged that administrative steps be taken to provide facilities for the lawful sale of gold where such mining took place.

Despite the many problems facing the mining industry, the mining sector was well geared to progressively meet the needs of our country for the future. This instilled confidence in our country's future economic growth.

Following this speech, I took the opportunity to present a gift to President Mugabe on behalf of the Chamber of Mines. Smiles and applause from all those in attendance made us joyful. I delivered my speech, and then I hosted a luncheon for President Mugabe and all the cabinet ministers. Afterwards, I requested that the President meet informally with as many members of the mining industry present at the AGM as was possible. Although this was an unusual request, the President agreed to do this, and I was very pleased.

In the opening remarks of my speech, I warmly thanked His Excellency, our State President, Robert Mugabe, for accepting my invitation to officially open the meeting, and I also thanked the many cabinet ministers who had graced us with their presence and sincerely welcomed the many delegates from the mining industry.

My speech went on to state that 1990–91 had been a year characterized by frustration, hope and continued resilience for the mining industry and for our country's economy as a whole. Early in April 1989, the government unveiled the broad principles of its investment guidelines, and in May, the Senior Minister of Finance, Economic Planning and Development, the Chamber of Mines, and our partners in the enterprise sector and government, attended the CBI Investment Conference in London. Although several potential investors viewed the government's investment guidelines as lacking in detail and specifics, it was generally accepted that Zimbabwe had made a very good first attempt at addressing the real problems facing the country. The Senior Minister of Finance, Economic Planning and Development expressed his desire to address Zimbabwe's economic problems when he presented his budget to Parliament in July 1990 and when he presented an economic policy statement in October 1990.

We in the mining industry recognized that the stage had been set for a determined thrust towards economic rejuvenation and growth. Jointly with government officials and, in some cases, with members of the enterprise sector, the Chamber of Mines assisted in the drive for investment in Zimbabwe with visits to Canada and Japan to elicit investments and to explain opportunities becoming available to potential investors. These incentives included improved dividend-remittability rights and an export-retention scheme, which encouraged mining businesses to look forward to the future with hope and optimism.

The publication of the most comprehensive document on the liberalization and economic-structural adjustment program in February 1991 generated increased optimism in the future of the mining industry in Zimbabwe. The question many people asked was whether the country would be able to follow through and implement the very well-defined objectives of the program. Fear of an ill-informed pubic for the success of the structural-adjustment program as a result of initial hardships during implementation was a potential threat viewed. I believed that it was incumbent upon all of us in business and in politics to communicate candidly the detailed implications of the program. We had to frankly state that all Zimbabweans would need to tighten their belts initially, as the situation was likely to be hard in the beginning. We had to prepare people for the inevitable hardships and so that they would understand and accept that such a course was unavoidable if Zimbabwe was to be progressive and competitive in the future.

The Chamber of Mines chose as its theme for 1991 "The Economic Structural Adjustment Program and the Mining Industry." We strongly believed that the success or failure of the program would depend to a large extent on the ability of those productive sectors manufacturing, agriculture and mining to generate the foreign currency needed to support it. The mining industry was a major part of those productive sectors since it generated 45 percent of Zimbabwe's yearly foreign currency earnings. Captains of our industry therefore needed to emphasize the positive and implementable aspects of the program rather than spending time discussing the shortfalls in the program. I, for one, did not see any plausible alternative economic model that could solve Zimbabwe's economic problems in the long run. Therefore, I urged all members of the mining industry to put their hands on the plough and make the program work. Inadequate foreign currency for the mining industry was the most important bottleneck inhibiting increases in production. In addition, the industry operated plants and machinery so antiquated that they belonged in a museum, resulting in increased engineering costs in almost all mines, largely as a result of increased downtime for machinery.

I was very pleased with the untiring efforts of the Reserve Bank of Zimbabwe in using the Minerals Marketing Corporation to negotiate with a consortium of British and European banks for a facility of US$75 million to overcome difficulties brought about by the lack of foreign currency in the mining industry. During the negotiations, I offered the consortium a special account of mining industry detailing the total revenue inflow to entire industry every month. This account would provide clear evidence that the mining industry would certainly be able to repay the facility. The consortium was very pleased by this offer, and finally approved that facility for the mining industry.

Fuel and transport costs continued to increase in Zimbabwe then. Any increase in input costs placed additional constraints on the viability of mining operations, particularly at a time when the industry was facing a significant downturn in commodities prices on the world market, over which the Zimbabwean mining industry was a price taker, with no influence whatsoever. The plan to increase in electricity prices on 1 November 1990 by 17.1 to 29 percent forced the mining industry to face further cost increases, as it was one of the largest consumers of electricity in Zimbabwe.

On 14 August 1990, the Chamber of Mines and the Reserve Bank of Zimbabwe concluded negotiations concerning the floor price of gold, which raised from $700 to $950 per ounce. For the first time in years, gold producers would receive a support price that actually recognized the cost of producing gold in Zimbabwe.

In July 1990, following a series of meetings between the Chamber of Mines and the Mine Workers Union, an agreement was reached to increase minimum wages in the industry by between 12 and 18 percent for workers of Grades 1 to 13. Employers in the mining industry were also allowed to give higher increases depending on their ability to pay.

With the implementation of free collective bargaining in 1991, I hoped that the cordial relations between the Mine Workers Union and the Zimbabwe Chamber of Mines would facilitate further speedy and realistic agreements guided by the spirit of the utmost good faith in negotiations, resulting in a viable industry with the possibility of creating new job opportunities to address the country's chronic unemployment. My speech at the Chamber of Mines AGM marked the end of my term as President of the Chamber of Mines, so listing all these positive developments gave me full satisfaction.

The future of the mining industry in Zimbabwe certainly looked positive, particularly for new investors, in light of various incentives that were put in place, especially the additional foreign currency schemes. The future of the market-based economic system adopted by government under the economic structural-adjustment program also looked bright. I was also hopeful that additional incentives would soon be considered for pre-1979 investors who had already contributed so much to Zimbabwe.

In my time as President of the Chamber of Mines, I thoroughly enjoyed the very good relations between the Chamber of Mines and the Ministry of Mines in Zimbabwe. Deliberations the Permanent Secretary for the Ministry of Mines and I had with the business community in Canada, as well as the very successful negotiations we mounted in the United Kingdom accompanied by the Minister of Mines and Deputy Governor of the Reserve Bank of Zimbabwe, resulted in a number of joint ventures that introduced new capital into the mining industry. Very positive and meaningful achievements indeed!

I welcomed the commercialization of the mining parastatals as part of the economic structural-adjustment program. I hoped that this would result in greater flexibility in the marketing of minerals, particularly those that were not in production when the Marketing Act was enacted. The viable future production of minerals such as uranium, platinum-group metals and diamonds required special market considerations.

The mining industry as a whole voiced its strong concerns to the Chamber of Mines about the amendments to the Mines and Minerals Act passed on 14 April 1991. At that time, the mining industry was one of the biggest taxpayers in the country. The industry paid rural tax to local authorities in the areas where mines were located, based on production, to provide for social, medical and school facilities in their surrounding communities. It must also be appreciated that about 30 percent of our gold production came from marginal mines and that our ore grades of both precious and base minerals were frequently low by world standards, so mines' viability was often balanced on a knife-edge. I expressed my hope that the Minister of Mines would fully appreciate their narrow margins and would take this issue into consideration in his consultation with the mining industry.

I expressed my great thanks to the Chamber of Mines staff for assisting me with the information I needed to carry out my job as President of the Chamber of Mines. I sincerely thanked all my colleagues in the mining industry as a whole for their support and cooperation. I enjoyed my term in office and truly hoped that I made meaningful contributions to the industry. I also assured President Mugabe of the mining industry's unwavering commitment to the progress of Zimbabwe. I was the first to admit that the industry might have been very conservative in changing its attitude in the past and advised my members and colleagues publicly and candidly that such an inward-looking attitude had to change in our environment. I had to tell President Mugabe that the men and women in the mining industry were dedicated to Zimbabwe and to its progress, because all of them wanted a bright future for themselves, their companies, their children and this country. If they criticized some of our national policies, they did so with good intentions. Most businesspeople in Zimbabwe's private sector believed then that the task of creating employment was not up to government alone; it was our collective responsibility. We all had to find a solution to it together by first having faith and trust in each other and in each other's intentions.

My achievements in everything I was deeply involved in during my lifetime happened quickly and were so beneficial to me. As I look back now, it seems that most of these achievements came to me as if someone were always standing beside me and causing everything to happen to me. In all I was involved in—whether they were political activities (characterized by great danger and the possibility of death), civil-service jobs (in Canada and in Zimbabwe), business management (in various organizations and companies) or elected office (as President of the

Zimbabwe Chamber of Mines)—I enjoyed very fast employment, fast promotions and speedy election to top positions.

The various speeches I made in Zimbabwe, South Africa, Canada, Japan, Malaysia, Switzerland and the United Kingdom all added to my great achievements. My very broad exposure to different situations taught me that God really loves all of us here on earth. He simply expects each of us to be fair, kind and loving to others, regardless of one's rank, colour, wealth or nationality. I am so grateful for having been so privileged to receive such a lesson.

→ TEN ←

International Awards

As I prepared for my retirement and early after retirement, I received a number of interesting awards and appointments from the International Biographical Centre in Cambridge, United Kingdom, and also from the American Biographical Institute in the United States.

These two International Biographical Institutions published four books in which they showed brief outlines of my various prior management and executive positions in business and government service. The four books are entitled:

- Great Minds of the 21st Century
- 500 Greatest Geniuses of the 21st Century
- Living Legends
- Dictionary of Interational Biography

In 2004, I was given the Living Legend Award by the International Biographical centre, Cambridge, United Kingdom. This was followed by my appointment as Business Management Advisor to the Director General of the International Biographical Centre, Cambridge, England, recognizing my expertise within the business community.

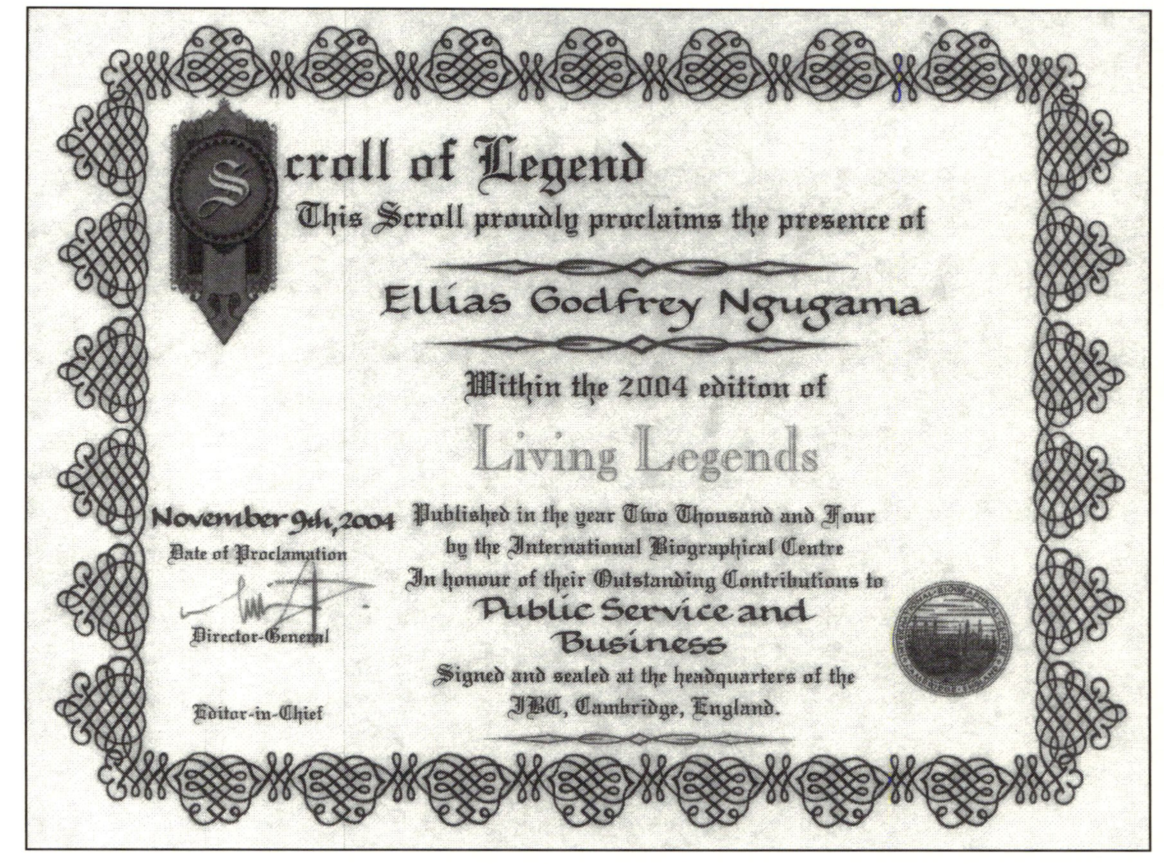

Scroll of Legend

This Scroll proudly proclaims the presence of

Ellias Godfrey Ngugama

Within the 2004 edition of

Living Legends

Published in the year Two Thousand and Four
by the International Biographical Centre
In honour of their Outstanding Contributions to

Public Service and Business

Signed and sealed at the headquarters of the
IBC, Cambridge, England.

November 9th, 2004
Date of Proclamation

Director-General

Editor-in-Chief

The International Biographical Centre, Cambridge, England Recognizes the expertise of

ELLIAS GODFREY NGUGAMA

within the Business Community

Furthermore, in accordance with the wishes of the Director General, the International Biographical Centre appoints the above mentioned

BUSINESS ADVISER

TO THE DIRECTOR GENERAL

It is noted that this advisory role be for a life tenure as the said adviser contributes to the knowledge and global presence of the International Biographical Centre in its archival library for researchers in and around the historic city of Cambridge, England. Let this inscription bear testament to the excellence and dedication available to the Director General as his desire for global awareness continues.

DIRECTOR GENERAL

Signed and Sealed at the International Biographical Centre Cambridge, England

June 2006

DATE

In 2006, I was given The International Business Award for significant contribution to business management and development, again by The International Biographical Centre, Cambridge, England. The American Biographical Institute in the United States also gave me an award that year for significant contributions to business management.

The American Biographical Institute further appointed me as Lifetime Deputy Governor for the American Biographical Institute Research Association.

I was also inducted into The International Biographical Centre Hall of Fame, in the field of business and public service.

GLOBAL YEAR OF BUSINESS - 2006 -

This certificate commemoration declares and confirms that
On the the Twenty-fifth Day of July 2006

Ellias Godfrey Ngugama

has been officially awarded

The International Business Award

for significant contributions to

Business Management and Development

Given under the hand and seal of the
International Biographical Centre,
Cambridge, England

Director General

Editor-in-Chief

Authorised Officer

PROCLAMATION

The Governing Board of Editors of the ABI
has selected

Ellias Godfrey Ngugama

as a

Great Mind of the 21st Century

due to significant accomplishments within, and mastery of

Business Management

As Documented in the 2005/2006 Edition of

Great Minds of the 21st Century

Reserved for Men and Women Whose Accomplishments and Influence are the Result of Superior Conditioning of the Intellect.

DATE *May 26, 2006*

Chairman

Vice Chairman

Managing Editor

Governing Board of Editors

Degree of Declaration
Ellias Godfrey Ngugama
Board of Governors
LIFETIME DEPUTY GOVERNOR
Inauguration 2006
American Biographical Institute
Research Association

IBC Hall of Fame

Ellias Godfrey Ngugama

Number 64 of 100

Sirs, I have the honour to
inform you that on
the 8th day of March 2006
the above named was inducted
into the
IBC Hall of Fame
for their outstanding
achievement in the field of:

Business and Public Service

Director General

There are four large books published by The International Biographical Centre and by the American Biographical Institute that provide brief descriptions of my various positions in a number of organizations.

All these awards from and publications by these international organizations have added so much to my personal achievements. I am grateful to the Almighty for rewarding me so plentifully.

ELEVEN

Highlights of Various Activities and Gatherings

My work as Chairman of Anglo American Corporation Zimbabwe was pleasing right from the start. Both the Chairman of Anglo American Corporation International and the retiring Chairman of Anglo American Corporation of Zimbabwe, whom I was replacing, attended the first meeting of the board of directors with me as Chairman. The following session photograph and news reports of my appointment are meaningful indeed.

PEOPLE

Ngugama assumes Amzim Chairmanship

New Amzim Chairman, Elias Ngugama

Anglo American Corporation Zimbabwe presented cash awards to top medical students following their final examinations in Medicine at the University of Zimbabwe. I have highlighted the presentations I made to two doctors who had achieved excellent results on their examinations.

In my presentation, I recognized Dr. Chirashe as the fourth woman in 26 years to achieve an honours degree at this university. Not only that, but she was the first Black woman to have achieved such wonderful results on her final examinations.

Both Dr. Chirashe and Dr. Ralph Nhiwatiwa achieved honours in medicine, Dr. Chirashe in medicine, pediatrics, surgery, and obstetrics and gynecology. I enjoyed giving the cash awards to these two doctors following each of their final years at the university.

Business Herald, Thursday September 20 1990 Page 17

Ralph Nhiwatiwa (left) one of recent winners of the Top Medical Award, being congratulated by Anglo manager Mr Elias Ngugama.

Dr Chirashe receiving her award from Mr Ngugama

I made various speeches as Chairman of the Organizational Training and Development Company (OTD). I often highlighted Zimbabwe's need for effective human resources in order to achieve our plans for structural adjustments to our economy.

Mr Ngugama opens the seminar with, seated from left, Mr Dahlin, OTD managing director Mr Keith Thomas and Mr Andersson

Effective human resources will help structural adjustment to succeed, says Ngugama

Mr Ngugama

When I became Chairman of Astra Corporation in Zimbabwe, following the successful development of the human resource programmes, I became involved in demerging the Corporation into three companies and their various subsidiaries. I then listed these companies on the Zimbabwe Stock Exchange, and they became very successful public companies in Zimbabwe.

Ngugama now chairman of Astra Corporation

Elias Ngugama

No. 67 / March 2000

Astra News

is a quarterly house publication for all Astra group companies in Zimbabwe

The Astra group of companies

Astra News

Astra Limited listed on the Zimbabwe Stock Exchange

A toast: Stuart Mattinson, Sagit Stockbrokers joint managing director, Tim Johnson, Astra Limited chief executive, Elias Ngugama, Astra Limited chairman, Emmanuel Munyukwi, ZSE chief executive

core activities namely earth moving, paints and foods, and improving viability.

When I retired as Chairman of Anglo American Corporation Zimbabwe, I thoroughly enjoyed my last board meeting and my farewell party, attended by a huge crowd. I have fond memories of these two occasions.

OPERATIONS

Elias Ngugama Retires As Amzim Chairman

Attending the last Amzim board meeting chaired by Elias Ngugama at Charter House (from left): Vincent Uren, Philip Baum, Ngoni Kudenga, Bill Nairn, James Maposa, Tony Devlin, Sydney Mtsambiwa, John McCarthy (Secretary), Elias Ngugama, Godfrey Gomwe, Alan Wishart and Hugh Kendrick (Group Financial Controller).

Elias Ngugama Retires

As Amzim Chairman

Retiring Amzim Chairman, Elias Ngugama, at the farewell party which was held in his honour in Harare

Elias Ngugama (left) and Philip Baum share ideas with Dr Charles Utete, the retired Chief Secretary to the President and Cabinet

When I was elected the first Black President of the Zimbabwe Chamber of Mines, I conducted several meetings in Zimbabwe, South Africa and the United Kingdom. I was the first person to invite the President of Zimbabwe, Robert Mugabe, to attend the Chamber of Mines Annual General Meeting, which he accepted. I was thoroughly impressed by his attendance and giving an opening speech.

The new Chamber of Mines president, Mr Ellias Ngugama

Ngugama is new Chamber of Mines President

The SA Foundation last night hosted a function in Johannesburg for a four-man business group from Zimbabwe and Zambia. From left are Confederation of Zimbabwe Industries president John Deary; foundation director-general Kurt von Schirnding; Zimbabwe Chamber of Mines president Elias Ngugama and Zimbabwe National Chamber of Commerce president Phil Jumbe. The group is on a three-day visit sponsored by the foundation. Picture: ROBERT BOTHA

Mr Ngugama presents a Chamber of Mines gift to President Mugabe at the Nyanga meeting

ABOUT THE AUTHOR

Ellias Ngugama is a retired business executive. Over his extensive career, he served in directorships to chairmanships of some of the largest multinational corporations and was also elected President of the Chamber of mines in Zimbabwe. In addition, Mr. Ngugama also enjoyed a successful career in government as Director of Finance and Administration in Canada, Deputy Comptroller and Auditor-General in Zimbabwe. Throughout his career, he presented various speeches in Canada, Japan, Malaysia, Switzerland, the United Kingdom, South Africa and Zimbabwe.

Manufactured by Amazon.ca
Bolton, ON